W9-CEN-467

AMERICAN
INDIAN
POTTER

By
Susan Peterson
Designed by DANA LEVY

KODANSHA INTERNATIONAL
Tokyo, New York and San Francisco

Distributed in the United States by Kodansha International/
USA, Ltd., through Harper & Row, Publishers, Inc., 10 East
53rd Street, New York, New York 10022. Published by
Kodansha International Ltd., 12-21, Otowa 2-chome,
Bunkyo-ku, Tokyo 112 and Kodansha International/USA,
Ltd., with offices at 10 East 53rd Street, New York 10022
and The Hearst Building, 5 Third Street, Suite 430, San
Francisco, California 94103.

ISBN 0-87011-685-1
ISBN 4-7700-1185-7 (in Japan)
LCC 84-80331

Library of Congress Cataloging in Publication Data

Peterson, Susan (Susan Harnly)
  Lucy M. Lewis, American Indian potter.

  Bibliography: p.
  Includes index.
  1. Lewis, Lucy M.   2. Acoma Indians—Biography.
3. Acoma Indians—Pottery.   4. Indians of North
America—New Mexico—Pottery.   I. Title.
E99.A16L496 1984   970.004′97 [B]   84–80331
ISBN 0-87011-685–1 (U.S.)

CONTENTS

To my parents,
and
to my children,
and
to everyone in the Lewis clan

Lucy M. Lewis wishes to dedicate this book
to her late husband, Toribio, father of her
children and grandfather of their children

FOREWORD

IF ONE WERE TO KNOW THE PUEBLO potters of New Mexico and Arizona, there are few accomplished potters of distinction, and one of them is Lucy Lewis of Acoma Pueblo, New Mexico. It was in Idyllwild, California while teaching at ISOMATA, University of Southern California's mountain campus for the School of Music and the Arts that I met Mrs. Lewis and her daughters Emma Lewis Mitchell and Delores Lewis Garcia, sharing with the world the clay traditions of Acoma Pueblo.

Quiet and modest, it is hard to see the lively creative energies blossoming in the soul of this serene grandmother from New Mexico. Dedicated to the innovation of the Acoma pottery traditions, she has learned her art well. The unique forms and decorations have appealed to fellow potters and the outside world, and her artistic career has received national and international recognition with exhibitions at the Smithsonian Institution, Washington, D.C., and the New Mexico State Governor's Award, to name but two of her honors.

Mrs. Lewis' unflagging faith to her traditions and arts will leave an everlasting influence on the history of her people, and she has given the Indian and non-Indian a poetry of clay images that will live always within us.

Fred Kabotie
Shungopavi
Second Mesa, Arizona

PREFACE

I AM ON A PILGRIMAGE OF MY OWN today. Ten years ago, in 1974, my book *Shoji Hamada, a Potter's Way and Work*, was published by Kodansha International. The research for that book was done several years before that at Mr. Hamada's home and workshop in the Japanese pottery village of Mashiko.

Many times I have returned to this village. Each short respite, before and after Mr. Hamada's death, has been significant. Here, also, is where I wrote the preface for my second book, *The Living Tradition of Maria Martinez*. That afternoon I talked about American Indian art with Mr. Hamada, and he had reiterated his conviction—which I first heard in 1952 after his visit to Santa Fe and Maria at San Ildefonso pueblo—that American Indian art is of great significance and represents an extraordinary contribution to the art of the world.

I am back in Mashiko again, at the inn where I first stayed more than a decade ago. The purpose of this visit to to slake my curiosity about the artistic and other changes that have occurred here and to indulge in a bit of nostalgia. For several years I have been traveling back and forth from Los Angeles and New York to the Acoma pueblo in New Mexico, the home of Lucy Lewis, writing, observing, and photographing her way of pottery. I am still involved in the quest Mr. Hamada set me on in our earliest conversations in 1952, a search for those artists who work within sophisticated folk traditions and who in our lifetime have embarked on special paths.

My mind juxtaposes, on the one hand, thirty years of experiencing Mr. Hamada's way and work and the areas of Japan and the many crafts and objects that he revealed to me with, on the other, the work and lives of native Americans whom I have known an equally long time. I note many similarities that permeate their living and working. For instance:

—Respect for and an intimate relationship with tradition.
—Strong personal value systems.
—Reverance for and importance given to art as part of daily life.

For American Indian or traditional Japanese craftspersons, everyday existence and the making of objects are often the same. It is interesting to note that some of us who have chosen to work in a contemporary idiom, whether living in the city or countryside, often take on parts or aspects of a more basic, "native" life-style as a means of personal fulfillment. Walking the pottery-shop lined streets of Mashiko today, I recall comments in the 1950s that the potters of this village had lost whatever they had once gained from Hamada's example. In those days I disagreed, feeling that the (then) fifty or so local potter families were making reasonably good wares. Today the number of potters has greatly increased, and industrial techniques have appeared in many workshops. New forms and colors are much too "tasty," to use Mr. Hamada's expression for work that is not pure. Sadly I agree that much of what I see now in this village lacks something. Spirit perhaps; nourishment certainly. It is likely that local potters do not go and renew themselves at the little museum Hamada built here to house his collection of work by unknown craftsmen of all times and places.

As the world turns, for a brief time, pure artistic influences come as comets, revitalizing traditions and fostering subtle innovations. Indifference and misunderstanding later appear to coagulate and clot the flow. Still, the works of those of innate wisdom and skill can endure as beacons to be seen and heeded again and again.

Lucy was nourished by the ancient potshards she found as a child on her mesa. She invested the work of her ancestors with her own voice and, in turn, influenced her people. It is my hope that this book will extend her realm and stimulate others.

The art of the native Americans is among the great traditions of the world. For the peoples of the Southwest of the United States, spinning and weaving, metalsmithing, and pottery are the important expressions. The rituals that form the basis of Pueblo life require pottery. In some places, potting is practiced almost exactly as it was long ago.

But it is a vanishing art, except for a few matriarchs of Lucy's stature, much as the folk traditions anywhere vanish in today's society and economy. The sacred clay is too hard to prospect, too difficult to pulverize and process; pigment rocks are scarce, and grinding them is arduous; cedar and dung firings demand much experience and skill; and who wants to paint designs with a stiff brush chewed from the midrib of a yucca leaf?

Of significance is the thread that runs through the folk art of all peoples. We must continue to preserve, in collections and documentations, the thought, the feeling, the warmth generated by objects and the making of objects that solve human needs. "I mix my clay with me," says Lucy. Her work jumps with the excitement of her belief.

The day will come when we no longer have any of these arts emerging from the strong, uninterrupted traditions in our midst. The legacy to which we must hold is the understanding of what that work stood for and is—an all-encompassing expression of the best that is human.

Mashiko, Japan
March, 1984

ACKNOWLEDGMENTS

THE LEWIS FAMILY TOLERATED MY presence. I know it was not easy for them—who value privacy and resist invasion—and at times my own ability to understand was also stretched, then expanded. My gratitude goes to all of them: the revered Lucy; Emma and her husband, Lee Mitchell, their children and grandchildren, who shared much of their life with me; Dolores and her children, whose warmth and generosity were of great help; Belle and her husband, Stan Lucero, who lent their collection of Lucy's pots for photographing; Andrew, whose fine recollections and wonderful paintings have greatly enhanced the book; Ivan and his wife, Rita, whose different life and way of pottery at Cochiti pueblo captured me; to all the grandchildren and some great-grandchildren, who shyly and willingly talked with me and who gave me sketches of their grandmother's pottery designs for this book; to all of you my profound thanks. This book is a compilation of everyone's conversations with me over several intense years, and of my own observations. And to those of the family who refused, thank you for teaching me.

I am always grateful to my children—Jill, Jan, and Taäg—for their patience and assistance. In this case Jan went with me to Acoma several times and took some of the photographs. My gratitude also to my parents, Dr. and Mrs. Paul Harnly, without whose kindness and understanding I would have more than normal difficulties.

Many others have helped, with insight or special aid: Santana and Adam Martinez and Barbara Gonzales and their families at San Ildefonso pueblo; Dr. Bertha P. Dutton; Fred and Michael Kabotie; Robert Schwarz, Jr.; Mildred Wolcow; Edna Norton; Katie Noe; Frank Harlow; Myles Libhart; Stewart Peckham; Barbara

Mauldin; Barbara Stanislawski; Michael Hering; Richard Sandoval; Bob Dahner; Arthur Olivas; Forrest Fenn; Rick Dillingham; Sam and Alfreda Maloof; Wendell Keith; Rose Slivka; Patricia Clark; Martha Benson; Rena Lupe Kohlmeyer; Mr. and Mrs. Wallace Holladay; my students and colleagues at Hunter College in New York City and at Idyllwild School of Music and the Arts in Idyllwild, California; and Laura Gilpin, posthumously, for all her photographs of native Americans and especially the ones she took of Lucy.

My appreciation is boundless for the people at Kodansha International, who produce thoughtful and beautiful books, and my thanks go especially to Saburo Nobuki, the Managing Director, to Tad Akaishi, who tolerates my caprices and whims in the Kodansha New York office, to Dana Levy, who knows how to design a book like few people do, and to the staffs of the Tokyo and New York offices.

A number of institutions have been willing to allow photographs of their collections of pottery or have provided photographs and archival material: Museum of Indian Arts and Laboratory of Anthropology, the School of American Research, Indian Arts Research Center, and the Photo Archives of the History Bureau of the Museum of New Mexico, all in Sante Fe; the Museum of Albuquerque, New Mexico; the Southwest Museum, Los Angeles; the Museum of the American Indian, and the Museum of Natural History, New York; the Library of Congress, the Smithsonian Institution, and the Indian Arts and Crafts Bureau, Washington, D.C.

Many gallery owners and traders have been helpful to the Lewis family and to me, and the various organizations that have honored Lucy in the past several years have also assisted me—particularly the people at Northwood Institute (Michigan) and at Octagon Center for the Arts (Ames, Iowa). No book of this kind is accomplished without many mentors and discussions, and I am grateful to everyone who has contributed to my life.

Susan Harnly Peterson
New York
March, 1984

LUCY M. LEWIS

THE SETTING

Approaching the acoma mesa, miles from the highway on a dirt and gravel road, the landscape is so quiet that the stillness is almost sound. Here the sky is far vaster than one can remember, and the land breathes out its immutability. Here there is peace.

Cloudless days reveal the profoundest blue at the zenith of the immaculate dome over the earth. Cumulus clouds are billows of light, their internal shadows the same blue as the sky. When rain or snow threaten, shafts of light explore rifts in the blue-black ceiling, or the foreboding blackness is offset by the glow of the sun hidden in another part of the sky.

In the early morning the mesas emerge pink, orange, lavender, iron red; in the afternoon a blue haze may cover the distant purple landscape, erasing the crisp outlines of morning. Sometimes the brightness of an afternoon turns just the right shade of soft gray and reveals a rainbow rising and disappearing or arching to touch the opposite horizon. Now and then, even when there has been no rain, a transparent rainbow appears in front of a mesa, like a curtain veiling the shimmering rock behind.

Occasionally the sunset turns the billowy mounds or sweeping wisps of cloud into blazes of yellows and pinks, changing, deepening, finally glowing the color of gold foil. Then the mesas are indigo silhouettes against the horizon, with fine edges of bright gold catching the rock faces or haloing the ridges.

This is the land of the Acoma Pueblo people and of the potter Lucy Lewis, whose traditional yet innovative transformations of earth and fire have influenced Pueblo work and life.

One reaches Acoma pueblo from Interstate 40 near Grants, New Mexico. The landscape is dotted with mesas. Some seem to hang in folds, curving from the top down like velvet and flowing to the ground; others stand stark, square, and vertical, pasted against the sky. The rock on top of which the Acoma people have lived for over a thousand years is not visible from the highway.

Turning off the freeway, one follows the faint hand-lettered signs that indicate the route. The road winds through low hills, past small adobe houses, animal corrals, and fields of corn. Strange sandstone formations spike the sky. Suddenly the stark, sheer rock of a mesa comes to view.

The Indian call it Katzimo, "Most Sacred Place," or Enchanted Mesa. Lucy's son Andrew, who has lived nearly all his life at the pueblo, has never climbed the rock, although he says that he has been urged to make the ascent. Climbing up is possible, Andrew says, but coming down is another thing. "Some people have been stuck up there and had to be rescued. It is only seven hundred feet long and fifty feet wide on top," Andrew stamps his foot for emphasis. "There is a story about the Indians looking up at that mesa from below, and thinking that there was gold up there because they could see yellow color. But they found it was just corn." Enchanted Mesa is important in the belief of the Acoma, and they prefer to respond to prying questions with indirect answers.

From the foot of Enchanted Mesa one can see the Acoma pueblo mesa beyond: larger, not quite as abrupt, darker because of vegetation, and softened somehow by the land rising in mounds at its foot. Indians and Anglos alike call it Sky City. Near the approach are clusters of craggy sandstone rocks spearing the open space, standing guard. Lucy's grandchildren recall playing in these rocks when they were youngsters, the good luck snakes they would find, and the hidden pond cisterns. It seems a long way from the foot of the mesa for a place to play.

The top of the rock, seen from this distance, undulates with the rhythm of the different rooftops. The adobe covering the walls of the houses comes from the surrounding land—the rock and the dwellings are the same dusty ochre color. The two towers of the church rise above the flat roofs. If one did not know there was a village here, it would be easy to miss.

There are small signs announcing Acoma pueblo and asking tourists to stop at the visitor center at the foot of the mesa to register and pay a camera fee. The shop sells Indian crafts; a delightful museum displays some of the history of this region and its people. Most visitors take a guided tour of the mesa in a van from the visitor center; no one is allowed to roam unattended.

Mount Taylor dominates the northern landscape. The Acomas used to cross to this mountain for herbs and for religious observances. It is also where the tall trees grow. *Vigas*—whole pines stripped of limbs and bark—used as ceiling beams in the church and the houses, were carried from that mountain, across the intervening hills and valleys, and up the mesa. No one knows quite how.

Big logs are still brought from Mount Taylor to the mesa for firewood, for cooking and heating. From the mesa, the land is devoid of trees as far as the eye can see. Except for brush, the gentle green and brown slopes of the hills are covered with grazing grass. It is hard to imagine the old days, when there were farms in the valley, when there were sheep, and when Mount Taylor was a normal run from the mesa for the goods it bestowed.

Rain in this land comes in flashes, immediate and hard, or in sheets. Often it is possible to stand on the dry side of a curtain of rain. The Pueblo people catch rain water—and probably have done so since the beginning of time—for washing their hair, for cooking, and for rituals, even if they live with utilities on the flat land down below the mesa.

Approaching Sky City at dusk, one sees scattered lights along the top. Now only nine to twelve families live there all the time, without electricity or running water. The religious leaders and their assistants are obliged to reside at the pueblo continuously for their year of service. Other members of the 150 families with houses on the mesa come and go, for ceremonies, for gatherings, and to sell pottery to the tourists who are allowed on the mesa during the day.

In winter the steep dirt road, with its one sharp curve four hundred feet above the valley, toward the top of the mesa, can become too icy to use. Then everyone walks, clinging to the ice-cold holes bored in the rock. Until a few years ago, when the road was built, the Acoma people used these hand- and foothold steps all the time. After Thanksgiving, snow covers the top of Mount Taylor, the mesas, and the valley below. Pottery can be made during less than half the year: two or three months in spring and summer, and two or three in autumn.

The mesa is five hundred feet high, and the area on top is seventy acres. Building facades face south. The two- and three-story dwellings in the center of the pueblo are terraced so they will be exposed to the winter sun even in its most southerly position. A high wall on the north side of the mesa acts as a wind shield. The buildings share common walls. There are paths in front and behind the houses and occasional alleys between them, which are often used for storage. Ladders of weathered pine logs punctuate the adobe buildings at various levels; the tallest ladders signify kivas.

Lucy's family house is at the far northwest corner of the mesa. It has been rebuilt several times. The lintels of the door and window are painted sky blue. Specks of golden straw flicker in the sun on the adobe facade. The screen door creaks when it is opened. To the left is a spectacular view, through the small space between buildings, of the valley below.

The first room inside is a sitting area, floored with linoleum over packed dirt; here is a couch, where Lucy sometimes sits to work pottery at an improvised table. By the adobe fireplace is a low stand with a checkered napkin covering, and on it a bowl of very finely ground cornmeal, a cup of milk, and a bowl of food morsels for the spirits. On the walls are pictures of Lucy and her grandchildren, of her son Andrew, of her late husband Toribio, and there is a rack of pollen pouches for ceremonial wear. A few early polychrome pots are on the mantle, kept for special use.

The kitchen is off to the left, large and sunny. When Lucy is here for lengths of time she sits at the big table, near the wood stove, making pots. Emma and Dolores mix clay for their mother, on hands and knees on the linoleum floor or with their feet. There is space for all three women to work in clay at this table—or for Andrew's pots when he is there alone—with room left over for everyone to eat. Deep window sills in thick adobe walls make fine places for stacking dried foods. There is no refrigeration; packages and cans fill boxes on the floor and sit on the shelves with plates, bowls, and cups. This kitchen frequently seats a number of visitors, at religious and festival times.

At the back of the house, facing north, is a large room the length of the other two rooms, used for sleeping and for hanging ceremonial costumes and accessories. Several Laura Gilpin black-and-white photographs of Lucy, hanging on a wall, prompt stories about the famous photographer walking all the way up the stone steps to the top of the mesa, carrying her 8×10 camera and gear. Pottery canteens for rituals are hung in a row, with a bow and arrow and feathers. Andrew's pots dry on a board by a window, and his clay mixing and screening equipment stand on a bench. Lucy sleeps on the couch near the back door, under the window looking north over the valley.

Near the stone stoop at the back of Lucy's house is the beginning of one of many old trails carved in the rock, leading down from the mesa to the valley. In some places the steps are just holes cut into the vertical rock. Little horned toads scamper in and out of these indentations. The old stone steps, where steps exist, were once about eight inches wide; they are worn now in concave curves. Ugly concrete has been poured on either side of the stones, widening but not leveling the steps. They are difficult to manage, but remain in use. Many other ways to the mesa are said to exist, but this is the simplest. It is well hidden in crevasses of rock, and you would not notice it if you did not know where to look.

The sun and the stars seem very close up here; you feel as if you could spread your arms and fly to the neighboring mesas. The air is still. No sounds reach the mesa from the workaday world far away, except when people arrive for the dances, and the beat of the drums reverberates in the emptiness. The people of the white rock have a long and secret history. Out of this place apart in the desert has come one of the great potters of our age.

1. Acoma pueblo—Sky City—atop a five-hundred-foot mesa, as seen from the access road.   2 (*overleaf*). Aerial view of the Acoma pueblo mesa.

3–6. The sky is vast in this country. Sunset light brings wondrous color changes to clouds and rock formations.

7. Enchanted Mesa, near Acoma pueblo.   8. Mountain junipers (called cedars locally) dot the landscape.   9. The rocks of Acoma mesa form dramatic silhouettes at sundown.

10. The fireplace in Lucy's "old house" at Sky City, with recent pottery by her son Andrew.   11, 12. Houses in the center of the mesa.   13. A neighbor takes her ease in the early morning sun.   14. Andrew's water-smoothed pots are ready for slip application and polishing; older ceremonial pots are on the sill.   15. Front window of Lucy's house with three of her pots.

16. Corn drying outside Lucy's house on the mesa.   17. Under the adobe facing, the drywall construction of the stone houses is revealed.   18. Sunrise and an adobe bread oven.

19–21. Old church on the mesa and adjacent cemetery.   **22.** At dawn.

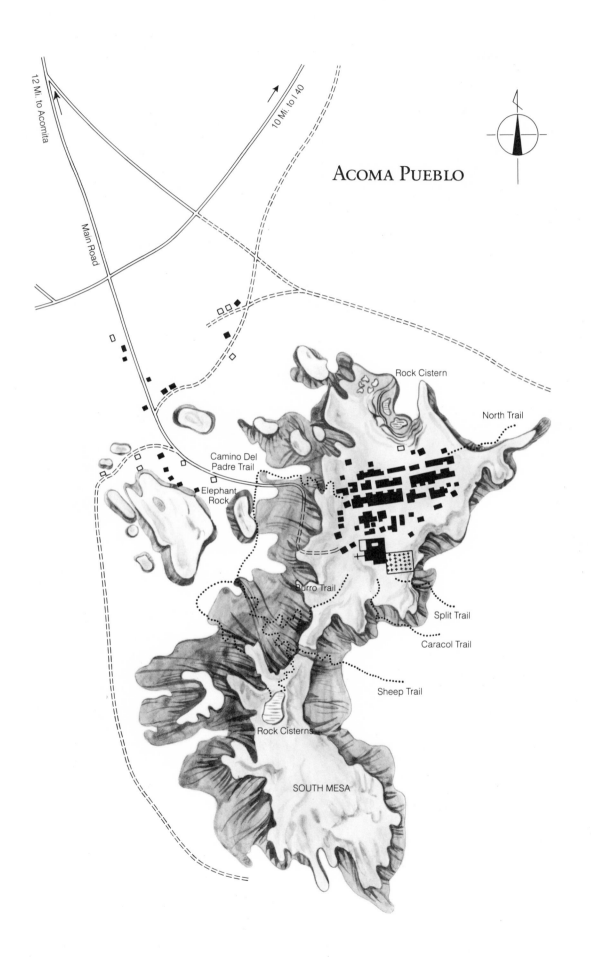

ACOMA PUEBLO

12 Mi. to Acomita

10 Mi. to I 40

Main Road

Rock Cistern

North Trail

Camino Del
Padre Trail

Elephant
Rock

Burro Trail

Split Trail

Caracol Trail

Sheep Trail

Rock Cisterns

SOUTH MESA

LUCY MARTIN LEWIS WAS BORN AT Sky City, probably in the 1890s. Lucy has no idea how old she is, or when her birthday really was, but she celebrates November 2. "An Acoma man," says one of her daughters, "asked me how old our mother is, and I said we don't know, we just guess. This man said 'I think your mother is two years older than I am, and I am eighty-one, born in 1902.' So maybe Lucy was born in 1900."

Ivan Lewis, her first child, relates it differently. He was born in 1919 and thinks that his mother was seventeen at the time. Lucy's daughters want her to be younger, so they can be younger. I had different answers each time I asked. One of the daughters tried to help and called the tribal office to see if there were any records, to no avail. It was suggested that we go to the Bureau of Indian Affairs office in Albuquerque or to the old church at San Fidel: "Someone must have a record." But in fact birthdays are unimportant to the Acoma, and they never keep records. Dates, numbers, and anniversaries do not exist except for tribal rituals. Her parents were Lola Santiago and Martin Ortiz. She cannot remember the names of her grandparents.

Lucy grew up on the mesa and did not go to school. She had two brothers, Joseph and Albert, who farmed and took care of the livestock with their father. Lucy helped in the home, took part in the ceremonial life of the village, and began as a youngster to make pottery in the traditional manner. According to Lucy herself—and everyone else I asked—the only influence on her as a potter was her great aunt, Helice Vallo.

Today Lucy has a sweet, old face. Her body is robust, and there is no obvious way to discern her age. You can see the wisdom of many years in her eyes, especially when she sits motionless and gazes at the distant mountains or into the air. Her face comes alive from total repose the moment she smiles.

In the 1960s, Lucy was struck by lightening during a storm at the house at Sky City. There was little hope that she would work again, but with perseverance she regained the use of her muscles and limbs. She walks without a cane, slowly and defiantly, as far as almost anyone else can, and she climbs into the cab of her family's big truck without assistance. She takes care of her own clothes and dresses herself, though she needs help plaiting her long braid. Her granite-gray hair is cut in the Acoma fashion, short of her ears on the sides and left long in back. It is said that the use of yucca as a shampoo keeps hair from turning white.

Lucy has a colorful wardrobe, and she changes clothes as the mood suits her. She has a number of bright shawls that she wears over her head, and one of the most charming articles of her everyday costume (as well as of ceremonial garb) is her apron, usually embroidered or trimmed in crocheted lace. She has boxes full of old Navajo, Zuni, and Santo Domingo jewelry. A wonderful jet was once mined at Acoma, and jewelry is said to have been made in the pueblo long ago. The tribe also kept sheep, until the government restricted the grazing lands for conservation, and the men were good weavers. Lucy speaks about the Acoma blankets she used to have, from her parents' time, but does not know what happened to them. She has been collecting jewelry all her life, is still acquiring pieces and giving them away to the children in her family as they begin to participate in the ceremonial life of the pueblo.

I have been coming to Acoma for four years, making the notes and photographs for this book, and I never cease to marvel at how much of these people's lives is devoted to traditional pursuits. Many days of preparation—food, costumes, learning—are required for every aspect of the frequent religious observances. Pottery making is sandwiched in somehow among the many duties and responsibilities of pueblo life. As a "venerable old one," Lucy's spiritual and healing role is particularly demanding. Anglos can never know just what these demands are, or understand the Indian's degree of commitment to them.

Because pottery is made only a few months of the year, and even then interspersed with other activities, I could expect to do just one or two things in each of my five-day visits. It took several trips to observe all the steps in mixing clay, many visits for the construction of the various pottery forms, and many more to document the painting. Between these sessions were hours of sitting at the table with Lucy, helping her to reconstruct the past.

One morning as we are eating Dolores' freshly made tortillas with butter and spam and eggs, I ask Lucy to tell me what it was like when she was a young girl up on the mesa. She smiles and begins to speak in Keresan, which one or the other daughter translates. "About all I remember is going to get water before the sun got too hot. Very early I went to get water at the cisterns. I had to make many trips, because our clay pots don't hold much—I went back and forth many times, bringing the water to the big storage jars in the house."

The girls nod at their mother's story; they also remember going after water when they were young, but acknowledge that it was more difficult in her day. Lucy smiles at her girls: "We used to spend most of the morning and maybe all day doing that, and then going to the storage pile for wood for the cookstove and the fireplace. It was my job to do those things. My father and brothers went down to the foot of the mesa to tend the burros or to the fields around the mesa where they dry-farmed. We didn't have irrigation for the wheat and corn. Sometimes the women went down below to help weed the vegetable gardens, but just getting the water was usually all a day would hold for me."

The calendar was based on solar observation, and still is for ceremonials. In Lucy's youth everything was planned according to the sun and the changing of the seasons. Her mother, she recalls, could not understand "why those people invented time that you could wear on your wrist," saying that the only right way was to go by the sun. The endless repetition of rituals, the lack of written language, the hardships of daily existence, and the subordinaton of time to the rhythms of nature make schedules (as we know them) of no importance. I recall Maria Martinez, the famous potter of San Ildefonso pueblo, telling me that if the good Lord gave me the next minute, that was time enough to decide what to do with it.

Grants, the nearest town to the pueblo (seventeen miles away), was a coal and pumice mining center. When the railroad was built, Lucy would go to Grants with her mother, leaving early in the morning with the horse to get to town by ten or eleven and sell pottery to the passengers. Lucy's father sometimes worked in a grocery store in Grants, and her mother would stay there, too, sending Lucy back home to make more pottery. Her mother made pots in Grants and sent them back with Lucy to fire at the old house on the mesa.

Acoma potters have been making pots of the native clay for the past several hundred years, in a variety of shapes, for ritual use and more lately for sale. Traditionally, a coating of polished white slip was covered with a busy painted decoration of bird-and-flower designs. Firing was accomplished by burning cow chips under and around the pots.

Lucy laughs, recalling the kind of pottery she made in those days, gesturing with her hands to show me several shapes and sizes. Her daughter exclaims, "I think I have some of those old ones you made," and runs to the cupboard, extracting two small pieces she brings to her mother. Eyes glowing, Lucy picks up each one and turns it slowly, as if she was making it again. Excitedly, in her own language, she speaks of the other pots she made for tourists. "I called the little bowls ash-bowls. They had twisted handles or bird heads and places for the cigarette. And I made Easter-bowls that were like baskets with scalloped edges, and I'd put cigarette places there, too."

Still fondling the pots Dolores brought—one a small vase with orange parrots and the other a shallow bird shape with a saucy tail and orange and black designs—Lucy says, "Boy, you can make millions of these easy, and they were easy to sell!" I know the uncharacteristic slang is probably her daughter's translation, but I am impressed. I ask how much she got for one of these at the time, sure that the answer would be five or ten cents, and it was.

"At that time, when you really needed to sell," Lucy continues, "you would go to the front of the train, where you got a head start with your basket of potteries. I always went where I would have first chance at the passengers. I charged seventy-five cents for the big jar, a tall one, and if I sold that I knew I had done really well." She holds her hands about nine inches apart to indicate the height of the vase.

Lucy always carried the pots in a basket on her head or in an enamel dishpan. Before I could complete my mental image of the young Lucy with a beautiful Indian basket full of pots on her head, she went on quickly: "Not an Indian basket, you know—a bushel basket, a grocery basket."

Her two daughters add another story. They remind their mother that she used to take them with her to sit by the roadside on Route 66 to sell pottery. As little girls they were allowed to do their own trading, rather than selling, for magazines or ice cream. Talking at once, they recall the man who used to come by with sweet potatoes, trading for little pots. "That was the first time we ever ate sweet potatoes!"

Sometime late in the 1910s Lucy married Toribio Luis, also called Haskaya. Nine of the children from this marriage, born between 1919 and 1947, are alive today. Of the girls, Emma and Dolores have the most affinity with their mother. Ivan, the oldest child and first son, married into another pueblo; he has lived at Cochiti for forty years and makes "storyteller" figures with his wife, Rita. Andrew, Lucy's second son and fourth child, lives in the old house at Sky City and takes an active role in the community. Ivan changed the spelling of the family name to Lewis when he went into the marines in World War II. Some of the grandchildren have indicated they would like to adopt an Indian surname—their grandfather's name, Haskaya—but everyone uses the formal Lewis appellation.

Andrew remembers that his mother and father worked in the garden together. Working with growing things is a sacred experience. "Dad planted the corn. White was for ceremonial use and for *pozole*. Blue corn was used for bread and mush, so heavy and thick that it could be put into a soup or just drunk. We also made it like a pita bread but thinner, big like a hotcake, sort of a hard corn bread to eat with red chili paste. Yellow corn was for cattle feed. My mother helped my father as much as possible."

"We'd gather dry cow dung, dad and mom and I, sometimes with my sisters, for firing the pottery," recalls Andrew, who has given me many clues to Lucy's early life. He was not sent away to school as early as Ivan and his older sisters were. "I helped dad with the cattle. We had a lot of cattle, and dad would sell or butcher ones that wouldn't calve anymore. Mom and dad had an account at the country store. They would get food and clothes, put them on a bill until the following fall, then sell the cows and pay the bill. If any money was left over, like a quarter or fifty cents, I'd get it. I'd keep it for two or three days. It gave me a good feeling to have that quarter; it came for something I'd worked for."

The cows in Acoma families go to the youngest daughter, because she is not as established as her older siblings, and, it is reasoned, that with parents advanced in age, the youngest girl has little security. Lucy's last child takes care of the cows and horses in the fields some distance from the mesa, with occasional help from her nephews. Acoma has a tribal herd of bulls used to improve the quality of the cattle. In 1933 the government restricted the use of grazing lands, to conserve land resources; this has created hardships, especially since the tribe then was no longer able to raise sheep.

Emma, the first daughter to return to the reservation to live, savors the memory of her mother's canning. "She mostly canned meat, chili, peaches, and apples. We used to have an orchard down below until the freeway went through it. Apple butter— Lucy made such good apple butter! She made fresh peach pies with sweet tortilla crust; you roll the tortilla out, fill half of it with fruit, fold it over, and bake."

"We didn't have running water below the mesa, any more than we did up on the mesa," Emma continues. "My dad went after the water for canning, hauling it in barrels from McCartys village, where the government put in a tank. We've only had water down here about ten years. Lately, since Lucy's been making so much pottery, she's quit canning altogether. But we have freezers. In the old days they used to dig a hole in the bank behind the house, make it like a little room, and there they would bury cabbages, carrots, beets to keep cool—even apples for winter eating. We had pigs, chickens, turkeys, cows, and a small herd of sheep when I was little. A cow was butchered when we needed, for canning or for jerky. Even today we make beef jerky."

"Lucy was always making pottery except in the long winter. Too cold. Then I used to see her crochet and cross-stitch embroider. Crocheting was for aprons and curtains for the windows. Lucy used to put lines of crocheting alternating with cotton all the way up dress-aprons for costumes. She made so many of those that she would give them away, or take them when she went to another pueblo to visit."

"She did everything," Emma maintains. "She gardened, raised chickens, turkeys, pigs; she dried meat; she had a flower garden, too. She made her clothes and our clothes, crocheted, did the Indian things, made pottery, and had a lot of babies. We remember, but we don't know how she did all that. Part of the time our father worked for the railroad and he was away. When Lucy made pottery it was all by herself—she never asked anyone for help."

Lucy's face becomes solemn, and she begins to speak in Keresan. I bring her back to English by asking if Toribio ever wanted to help with the pottery. "No," she replies. "He went for clay, though. And he would get off his horse if he saw a pottery shard out on the range. He gathered the cow dung with the wagon, but he didn't help paint. I made big pots in those days for ceremonials, and little ones to sell."

Lucy's thoughts seem deep in the past. She looks up, bright-eyed, and recalls the time soon after Ivan was born, when her brother Joseph was babysitting while she went out to ready the ground for the firing of some platters. Ivan was crawling; Joseph was to watch him while Lucy built the pit. When she returned to the house for the pieces, every one was shattered. Lucy says Ivan got a spanking, and her sleeping brother was not even scolded. Today she says she would know which was the one to punish!

Her daughters laugh with her. They have heard this story before, they admit, because the thin walls of Lucy's pots have been the subject of many conversations. Usually, however, they conclude that it is perfectionist Lucy's own fault when pieces break before they are fired, because she is pushing too hard on the thin wall or scraping with too much vigor. All the children are taught from the very beginning to leave the pottery alone, and especially not to touch the tempting shiny polished pots. The cats and kittens, I notice, are not always so controlled.

Eventually trains made occasional stops at McCartys and Acomita, not only at Grants; then pottery could be sold to the tourists closer to home. "Sometimes we would go in the wagon to Laguna pueblo, where there was an old hotel and a hospital. They would give us a meal if we came to sell pots. It was a long way to go, but we used to like to do that," Lucy recounts, looking shyly up with a tiny grin.

The conversation at the table has been going on for a long time. Dolores leaves and returns with a large plastic bag in her arms. Setting it down in front of her mother, she empties the contents. "Look what I bought yesterday from a shepherder, all these pot shards," she says, moving them around with her fingers. Lucy immediately picks up the fragments with fine-line painting or corrugated textures and begins to separate them, saying, "See how many different patterns they had? Those old people! See how nothing is the same, these are all pieces from different pots. How wonderful to have so much difference!"

One of Dolores' children, getting ready for the school bus, kisses her grandmother as she leaves the house. Lucy did not go to school; her mother was very strict and kept her at home. Her daughters say that Lucy knew her own children should be exposed to the world outside, because she did not have the chance at all until she became known for her pottery. She sent all her children out to school, which had to be away from the pueblo. Almost all of them graduated from high school, and some have more education than that. "We gave our children the same opportunity too," states Dolores. "Our children know what's going on in the world."

"Some of these teenagers have been at receptions for their grandmother, so they have seen what goes on in the Anglo society. If it wasn't for Lucy, we—Emma and I— wouldn't be where we are today, and our children wouldn't have these experiences. We wish Lucy's mother could have known to give her that exposure, school and all, so that she could communicate. A lot of people want to talk to her, but she is too shy to talk back."

Emma agrees. She notes that all but the last of Lucy's children were born before Lucy herself had traveled farther away from the pueblo than Grants. The children were sent to school in Santa Fe and other places. Most of them have told me that their mother seemed to have an intuitive sense about the need for their generation to have contact with Anglo thought.

Other Pueblo people, those who know her or know about her, have discussed Lucy with me. All seem in awe of her determination and willingness to take risks. In the face of pressure from the pueblo not to sign pottery, Lucy began to sign her pots when she decided to enter the competition at the annual Gallup Intertribal Ceremonial in 1950, where she won a blue ribbon. At that time her last child was three years old. Whether from economic necessity or from a desire to have outside recognition of her work, Lucy had taken a big step. Later she was influential in getting Marie Chino, Jessie Garcia, and other important Acoma potters to follow her lead.

After the Gallup prize, Lucy's abilities slowly began to be recognized. One of her benefactors was Katie Noe, owner of a shop in Gallup, the first trader to buy Lucy's pottery. Emma remembers being with her mother once when Lucy had just sold a group of pieces to Miss Noe. Admiring the pots one by one, she pointed a finger at Lucy and predicted, "You are going to be real famous one day!" Lucy just looked at the floor, Emma relates, and said: "Oh, you are the only one who thinks that, and you're just telling me to make me feel good." Katie Noe tried again to make Lucy understand how good she was, but the modest potter was not to be convinced. "Lucy was perfect from the start," says Katie.

"We were all poor," Dolores acknowledges, "but my mom and dad eventually got an automobile so Lucy could take some of the ladies to the Gallup Intertribal or to Santa Fe. We never heard of this before about 1950 though. Acoma people didn't exhibit early. White people bought and maybe they exhibited our things—I think they did do that—but mother hadn't thought to go to shows."

"No famous person ever came to Acoma. Important people went to Santa Fe; it was the capitol, it had the Governor's Palace. And San Ildefonso is very close to Santa Fe. Maria went to places all over the country, and people came from all over to see her. We know that now."

"Our mother didn't have any way to do that. Lucy didn't sign her name on pottery until Gallup in 1950. She just used to put 'Acoma, New Mexico' on the bottom. That Rockefeller, Hewitt, Chapman—they always went to San Ildefonso, but never came to Acoma."

Emma's voice is strong, but about to break as she speaks. She has left unsaid, and I think she realizes, that Lucy and the other fine potters of Acoma developed without outside help and public recognition. The earliest pot of Lucy's that I have seen, dated between 1920 and 1930 by the Laboratory of Anthropology in Santa Fe, is as fine as anything she made later and in a different style. Her skills and her eye came to her naturally; recognition came much later.

Lucy met Dr. Kenneth Chapman, then the artistic director of the New Mexico Museum, when Laura Gilpin took her to Santa Fe in 1958. Chapman, who had influenced Maria and Julian Martinez in the 1920s, showed her ancient pottery, particularly Mimbres, Mesa Verde, Chaco Canyon, and told her these pots were her heritage. She had already been doing fine-line decorations for a long time, making up her own patterns from what she saw of the black hatching on gray shards she found on and around the mesa.

"Our mother got the Indian Arts Foundation award sometime, before there was an Indian Market in Santa Fe like now, and she got the Maria Martinez award from them, too," boasts Dolores shyly. "Lucy has always been proud of the honors she received. She was the first one at Acoma to show her work. Before, she never thought of her pottery as that kind of thing. But our father died in 1966, and that made it hard for her. Ivan was already at Cochiti, and Andrew lived away, so she had even more to do."

Lucy and the girls are suddenly very serious, and their voices lower; they are discussing the role of women and the changes that are taking place in pueblo life. I add that I read that pottery and basketry were ritual processes and that these skills were fulfillments for women. Now even this is dying.

41

Roles were more clearly defined in earlier days, they agree. A woman's life changes if she goes outside to work. Receiving money is different from trading. Bartering used to be the only form of exchange. Not only money, but time, is important. It never mattered before. Their culture is changing, and the only thing they know to do about it is to hang on to as many of their traditions as they can. All three concur that one of the most important aspects of pueblo life that has not changed is the mixture of all ages, young and old, at celebrations and in the home as well.

"There was a time a long time ago when Acoma pottery had almost died out. Lucy revived it; she kept it going," claims Dolores, mindful of the traditions we have been discussing. "When the freeway came through, that ruined it for everybody. We couldn't sit along the freeway like we used to sit on the two-lane highway, to sell our pots. Pottery died away, but Lucy was still going. People were coming to her to get things, and that helped the other women, too."

"We saw photos of Mimbres pots for the first time in the late fifties. Andrew Johnston at the Primitive Shop in Old Town, Albuquerque, showed us postcards and a book of Mimbres pottery and we copied the designs. Lucy had been doing fine-line designs much earlier, you remember, from the shards. People liked it. She had developed several different ways of doing those lines; she worked it out herself. Some of her designs were similar to the Mimbres ones, and when she saw those she went on developing more of her own. Now everybody does her style, and a few have worked out their own. It's exciting that many women are making pottery, but of course it makes it hard to sell, too." Dolores ventures a frown, following it with a smile.

"Father had a sister named Dolores; she was a great potter. They used to make a lot, I mean a lot. And the other sister, Lupe, would burnish the pots, and I think outline the design. They would fire four at a time. It took a bunch of manure! I remember my aunt made a pot about three feet high and two feet wide and they spread out a white manta [traditional dress] on the floor to carry the pot with. I don't even know how they got it out the door and took it to the pit and piled that manure up around. After that I don't even remember if it came out or not, but there's good potters on both sides of our family. Of course no one makes big pots like that now—no need of anything that big for storage, or even for ceremonies. It's too bad we don't have any of those old pots."

Dolores waves her hand. "You know," she says, "a good many people—museum directors, gallery owners—say that Lucy Lewis and Maria Martinez are too famous, that there are hundreds of good potters in Acoma and San Ildefonso and the other pueblos. That's true, but none is as good, as good with the public—none has done it as well or as long as Lucy and Maria. Some are younger, I know, and they have a way to go! I feel that it is these famous ones who had more skill, who worked harder, and publicized it by winning prizes, by being out there in public."

Pleased with that summing-up, Lucy and I take each other's hands across the table. "If we had glasses we could make a toast to Lucy," adds Emma. I have the last word: Lucy was shy when she was a girl and she still is. And at eighty-some years old, she is still growing as an artist.

LIFE AT ACOMA

T HE "ROCK OF AKU," CALLED SKY CITY, was first reported to the European world by Francisco Vázquez de Coronado, whose expedition encountered the forbidding mesa in 1540. He recorded that he found a mesa with a village on top, "the strongest position ever seen in the world," and named it Acuco, meaning "People of the White Rock" in Keresan.

The subsequent history of the pueblo and its relations with the Spanish is not pleasant. Acoma was the only pueblo to consistently resist the foreign enemy, as it had previously resisted encroachment by other Indian tribes: the bare flat summit of the rock—seventy acres of it, split by a narrow, deep cleft—was capable of withstanding long sieges. After Coronado came others intent on subjugation. Acoma earned a reputation as the most intractable of all the pueblos, but in 1599, Vincente de Zaldivar and other soldiers under Juan de Oñate killed six hundred Acomas and imprisoned six hundred more.

In 1680, the Indian Rebellion drove the Spanish back to Mexico, but they renewed their conquest in 1692. They promised forgiveness to all the pueblos that submitted to Spanish rule; Acoma held out again, the only one of all the pueblos, but succumbed in 1699. The Acomas took their religious practices and beliefs underground, outwardly submitting to the Church of the Spanish fathers. In 1848, New Mexico was ceded to the United States, and it became a state in 1912.

In 1863, a delegation of the governors of seven pueblos, including Acoma, paid a visit to President Abraham Lincoln, following the government's confirmation of the rights of the Indian tribes to own land. Lincoln presented each with a silver-headed cane as a token of the pueblos' right to self-government. The Acoma cane is engraved:

> A. Lincoln
> Prst., U.S.A.
> Acoma 1863

The cane, passed from one governor of the pueblo to the next as he accepts his office each January, signifies his right to the position.

In 1692, under the leadership of Father Ramirez, a Franciscan, a great church was erected on the southeast side of the mesa at tremendous hardship to the Indians. There was no access to the mesa except the foot- and handholds carved in the rock. The Indians carried a thousand trees and fifteen tons of rock to the top for the church, from Mount Taylor and from other distant places. A Mexican silver bell was bought at the price of a number of young Acoma girls; Andrew says that there is a place in Mexico that is full of Indians of his own heritage.

Catholicism is recognized but has little influence on the religious life of the community. At Acoma a priest plays no part in the daily life of the village. Every Acoma has a Spanish name, but unlike other pueblos along the Rio Grande, they do not speak Spanish. The atrocities perpetrated on the Acoma by the Spanish in the late sixteenth century and later are difficult to imagine, even when one reads the records of the events. Hostility encountered towards Anglos today finds firm roots in the brutal events of the Spanish conquest.

Of the nineteen northern and southern pueblos, six besides Acoma speak the Keresan language. The language has no written form. But in 1972, according to Andrew, a few textbooks were begun in Keresan, written phonetically. He tells of the experimental bilingual classes in the school at Acomita, to help young people and adults learn their own language. Permission was granted by the tribe; people with clear enunciation of Acoma helped develop a standard written form. Andrew is proud of the pueblo for doing this, because so many children speak English at home. He thinks that Acoma is the only pueblo to have authorized a written version of its own language.

I have often encountered people from various pueblos who distrust attempts to put their own languages in writing for fear of the mistakes and sacrifices implicit in the written word. From one perspective, this attitude is right. I finally was able to go to the January 23 feast at San Ildefonso. The deer and buffalo dancers had been in the kiva for many days prior to the performance, learning. Writing can record words, certainly, but cannot fully transmit an oral tradition. Voice, emphasis, tone, rhythm, facial expression, gesture, atmosphere, and many other things all convey meaning and nuance. Constant and continuous personal contact, rather than the written word, is perhaps one factor at the heart of the identity and longevity of the Pueblo people. For-mulizing things in writing will introduce a new force into Pueblo life. While the Pueblo languages have not had written forms, the people have had each other.

Acoma vies with Oraibi, the ancient Hopi village in Arizona, for the distinction of being the oldest settlement in North America. A sign at the botton of the mesa asserts that Acoma has been inhabited since A.D. 600; archeologists agree that it is at least one thousand years old. Today the population of Sky City, the two villages, and those who return for the census, is 5,500. Only a few families live on top of the mesa perma-nently, including the spiritual leaders. The rest are elsewhere on the reservation or in the nearby villages down below, but return to the mesa for the ceremonials.

Ethnologists believe that the Acoma people came to this valley from Mesa Verde, first to Enchanted Mesa and others, then to the mesa everyone calls Sky City. The Indians chose that name because they felt they were living close to the heavens. The early builders were fine engineers, say the present-day Acoma, positioning the house and windows to have sun during the winter, building the fireplace so there was no downdraft, using mica for window covering but leaving a hole to look out at the weather, and framing doors and windows with hand-carved wooden lintels. In the spring, the cisterns were cleaned, but the air was pure in those days and so was the rain.

In the center of the mesa, and running its length, are three parallel rows of com-munal buildings of two or three stories each, facing south. The stone to build these dwellings was carried up from the basalt beds in the valley, below the mesa and miles away. All the earth for the adobe surfacing had to be carried in hide bags from the plain, up the tortuous trails carved into the rock.

The only water came from rainfall collected in natural basins in the bedrock. The largest of such cisterns, down the south side of the mesa, is sacred and secret, not to be visited by strangers. In the old days the Pueblo people swept the space around it to keep it clean. Edward Sheriff Curtis, master photographer of the Indians, leaves us a number of images of this waterhole. Now the cisterns are dry from lack of rain, and each family brings water up from the valley in its own way.

In these rainwater cisterns, the women did the washing, beating the clothes against the rocks. They used rainwater for cooking and drinking, too. Now most women go to Grants or Albuquerque to do laundry. In the old days, Lucy's children say, in order to heat water, houses had a small hole in the roof on the first or second floor; sunlight would directly hit a pan of water placed below, for washing or bathing.

"Now children and tourists throw trash in our cisterns," Dolores contends. "That's one reason we bring water up from the village down below. We store it in big tanks here, but, you know, even that doesn't keep long."

Emma, Dolores, and I stand on the old church steps, on the high south side of the mesa, looking across the cemetery with its small white crosses and plastic flowers. "We keep using it over and over," says Dolores. The painted adobe sentries standing guard on the top of each pedestal and the adobe wall surrounding the graveyard breathe an ancient loneliness. There is a whisper of soft wind, a blue mist tints the sur-rounding mountains. All the caves and folds of earth on the mounds across the valley are sacred places and forbidden to the Anglo. The serenity is mysterious and eerie.

The inside of the church is a vast cavern. I have been here many times over the years; sometimes it is totally vacant, without color, without decoration, without even the few battered wooden pews, which are moved frequently. The ceiling is a lattice-work of split pine trunks. I have seen the big wooden screen behind the altar brilliantly painted floor to ceiling in Christian figures, and I have seen it plain. The girls say there used to be a huge painting on one wall, and they always wonder where it is.

Sometimes there are a few rows of pews near the altar; what remains is open hard-packed dirt floor, almost as smooth as stone. On the wall, behind glass in a small, narrow frame, is a short newspaper account of Acoma history. "We can have dances in here, sometimes do," remarks Dolores as she motions with her arms at the floors, the walls, the ceiling. The quiet blue of the sky and the gray-white clouds, visible through the windows near the roof, reinforce the strange calm. There is no one else here.

Lucy raised some of her family at Sky City; some of them stayed on the mesa with relatives when she was not there. Eventually she and Toribio moved down to McCartys village, to their first "old house" down below; even so, much time was spent on the mesa in rituals, ceremonies, celebrations, feasts. Today it is the same. The family moves up to the mesa several times a month for the "doings" and sometimes stays to make pottery.

In the old days, the men—and occasionally the women—went down to the valley to farm. The men would go for wood with the donkeys; they would get clay with a donkey and a travois. They brought the cow chips for the firings, too. The women generally stayed up on the mesa, making pottery, and never went anywhere, Lucy remembers. They also used to weave and do baskets. "Now they have stopped weaving and making baskets, they don't want to be 'Indians,'" she says, shaking her head slightly.

Dolores and Emma agree that it is sad to have lost those arts. "What with no running water and no electricity, it is sure hard up here," says Dolores, "but somehow when people are here it is really lit up!"

Lucy's current house is not the first she lived in on the mesa, but was rebuilt on the same spot about thirty years ago. Andrew lives in it full time; on the walls hang his trophies, old photographs, eagle feathers, headdresses, hunting bows, ceremonial canteens, and other ritual objects.

Houses are repaired when necessary. Some house foundations may be as much as six hundred years old—or more? Interior walls are redone more frequently. The first treatment is a layer of clay and straw; when it dries, a white clay is applied, which Lucy says is almost like the white slip she uses for polishing on the pottery; over this goes a limestone whitewash, freshened on special occasions.

Over the past six months a general change has been taking place in the facades on the mesa. The oldest core of three-tiered dwellings, running the center length of the pueblo, is being refurbished: new adobe surfaces, new lintels and ladders, a fresh coat of paint on the wooden window sashes, and new window glass. But the old buildings, crumbling as they were, were much more in harmony with the landscape, and I am sad on that account to see the renovation.

The ancient paths from the valley to the top of the mesa, much of which are a per-pendicular series of foot- and handholds carved in the rock, are not so difficult to climb up or down unencumbered. However, to have carried logs and rock for house construction up this way must have been harrowing. There was at least one burro path, but even that was too steep for burdened animals. The bumpy dirt road to the top of the mesa was constructed in about 1977.

Musing as we walk slowly in the dusty paths between the rows of dwellings, Emma says: "The old folks used to know each other by their Indian names; now it is another world. There were no Johns, Phils, Steves, and so on, then. Now Acoma children go to college and all that, but may have no respect for the older ones. It's really different now. It was so nice then. When you saw old people you would greet them— hello grandma, hello uncle—even if they weren't your relatives. Then too, people would take their caps off when they passed a shrine."

"What is a shrine?" I ask. "That's all I'm going to tell you," says Emma.

"We believe the sun has a spirit, and helps us," claims Andrew. "We believe all crops have spirit; my dad would talk to them. The same with animals. He would talk to them and he believed they had spirits; he would encourage them. When I was young, I thought a lot of things the old folks did were crazy. Now I don't."

"The oldtimers knew when to hunt deer and when not to hunt deer. The sun was the calendar; there are landmarks in the valley and on the mesa, for the sun and the moon. The moon has a role too." Indians had no clocks before their associations with Anglos. Even today the Pueblo people honor the natural clocks—the change of seasons, movements of herds, flights of birds, cycles of the moon, how many winters a person has seen. Winter is survival time, so they thought of it as the measure of a person's age. The greatest power in creation is the sun, they believe, for it determines all seasons.

Andrew continues. "The three most important elements are earth, light, and water. We think water is sacred. Rain used to be the only source for water, in the cisterns. The women carried water in their beautiful pots, on their heads. Lucy did that, she told me, but later it was just in pans, except for ceremonies."

"There was a boy, a Tewa, who came to Acoma. We talked about our religious ceremonies; his were different. The prayer we pray first is to Mother Earth. We make our own cornmeal for the blessing and keep it in an open bowl in the house. The three-step kind of bowl is for the medicine man's cornmeal. You just grind a few kernels at a time; too much and it will get worms. We use the same white corn for tamales as for prayers. Soak the corn in lime or lye, then grind it on a metate when it's dry. If you want to just dry corn, soak it overnight, rub off the hulls, lay it out to dry, and clean it again."

"We use pollen pouches for praying, too. It is good to bless yourself before speaking, and to use pollen for praying to the four directions. We take cornmeal and say prayers to the sun and the spirits, asking them to guard us. We get up early for health. We get fresh air. We say prayers to Mother Earth to help make things grow, and we pray to the sun for light and warmth," Andrew explains.

Dolores nods and says that Lucy used to tell her and Emma to "fix your feathers and go over to the church where she [some special relative] is buried and ask her to help you be as good as she was in pottery. So we would." Dolores explained that prayer feathers are made of domesticated and wild bird feathers put together in a certain way.

"If they wear out, make another. We don't take prayers from books; we just talk. You could just use cornmeal or pollen, but if you need real help, use all of them. Each one serves a purpose."

"We cover everything in our prayers. We pray for crops, for corn and squash and beans and so forth. We thank Mother Earth for giving birth to those seeds for everybody, not just Indians. We pray for peace and that no harm will come to our country. We have different places for different prayers, all around the mesa," says Andrew.

Certain times also have special significance. "For instance, after a baby is born, several events take place before the sun comes up; exactly when is very important. The parents choose a couple they wish to be sponsors for the child. The parents must be prepared, with feathers and prayers. The feathers and all are given to the sponsors, and the parents ask them to keep the child safe, like a godchild, but in Acoma tradition. We still do both ways, Catholic and Indian. The new child is held up in the sunrise to the east."

"The baby's cradleboard is made of wood, especially pine that was struck by lightening—which means struck by God. The mother can pass it down, maybe to the sponsors." Dolores reminds me that I have seen many babies in the pueblo wrapped up and strapped to cradleboards.

"The sponsors should come to the house to see how the baby is doing and to help the child as he or she is growing up. They teach how to plant the corn if it is a boy, or if it is a girl they teach how to make bread and pottery. They teach all the time when the child is growing up, until at least the age of eighteen or nineteen. Sponsors for a bride and groom have a different task, but it is still to help, for all their lives." Dolores pauses, and Emma goes on: "To be sponsors for a married couple or for a baby, they have to have had no problems, to be really good people, to be examples. That honor is bestowed so they can counsel."

"When a child is born, we give pottery to the other children in the village who have been good. There are many other times when pottery is given away. Girls get big pots; boys get canteens. If you are good, you may get pottery on every special occasion. Boys also get bows and arrows. These used to be used for hunting, of course, but now they are given as toys. There were rabbit sticks, too, with a weight on the end, for hunting. We also used the boomerang. These were important in life; now they are for play. For girls there are dolls; in the old days there weren't any. But the things we were given had significance, and that continues."

"Weddings are arranged by the bride's family, just like yours, and the parents set the date. It's really a small pueblo, so everyone knows. People bring corn to plant, or wheat—to start married life, they say. Usually they have both ceremonies, Indian and church. Practically the whole pueblo gets together, to butcher, bake, and fix all kinds of food. Everybody can help and everybody's invited. The sponsors are important and they do many things for the wedding, including give money. They have to keep the married couple in line for the rest of their lives," the girls emphasize.

Family relationships seem to be close, although there is also a separateness that is hard to find in our noncommunal society. Uncles, aunts, and other relatives may live with the family, and grandparents are always important. Children call nonfamily members by endearing terms such as aunt, uncle, or grandma. All the children may

23 (*preceding page*). Foot trail up Acoma mesa, 1899.

24. A feast day at Acoma, 1926.

25. Another trail up the mesa, 1926.

26. Acoma pueblo, ca. 1900.

27. Dancers leaving a kiva on a ceremonial day, ca. 1900.

28. Acoma women with water jars, 1926.

29. Acoma women fill water jars at the sacred cistern, Acoma pueblo, ca. 1890.

30. Father and daughter, Acoma pueblo, ca. 1890.

31. Dancers, Acoma pueblo, ca. 1900.

32. Tablita dance, Acoma, ca. 1900.

33. The church on the mesa, ca. 1900.

34. Finished pots and pottery in process. This is reputedly Lucy's family house, now rebuilt, at Acoma pueblo, ca. 1900.

35. Church bell, 1926.

36. Acoma pueblo, 1983.

remain in the family home, married or not married, and often the children of unmarried parents are cared for by the grandmother.

"When the first son in born," says Andrew, "the grandfather takes the baby out to put his feet in the first snow, to develop manhood." He remembers his father doing this with Leland, Emma's first son, and his own late uncle picking him up and suddenly throwing him into a snowdrift. He thinks he was about five or six, but he remembers.

In this pueblo, clan membership is matrilineal. The Acoma people used to have many clans, but some of them have died out, and now there are only about sixteen. "Our father belonged to the parrot clan, but Lucy belonged to the roadrunner clan, so we are roadrunners," explains Andrew, who knows most about these things. "The antelope clan has a major role in our tribe. If a family wants to acquire land it has to ask the antelope clan to see if it is possible; you go through channels. Once you build a house it is yours, but the land is the tribe's and you can pass it on, probably to a girl in the family."

"The antelope clan chooses the tribal officials after Christmas, at the end of the year. In Acoma we call the meeting house where the clans get together to choose 'the White House,'" he laughs. "The elected field chief circles the mesa every morning at dawn," adds Dolores, "wearing a blanket so people will know what he represents. He prays for all mankind." I mention that I have witnessed this on several early mornings and have seen the chief stop to stand silently on certain rocks jutting out over the valley, then continue his round. "There are a lot of shrines," Dolores concedes.

"There are four seasons, four directions, four days for fasting, four for weddings: four is a special number," Andrew continues. "For the religious ceremonies we observe the sun. When the January sun moves north, we go to the kivas together at a certain time. We have a lot of rituals; in June there is a big one, in July another, and in September one that Anglos can watch, when the crops are starting to ripen. That's when we thank the spirits for letting those things grow; we thank Mother Earth for food. In early October is another ceremony, the same as in July. In December is the winter solstice ceremony, when the sun has traveled farthest south; you people can see this one, too."

"Of course we have special rituals, too, that don't involve long dances. For instance, in the spring the field chiefs plant corn and the boys participate. Young girls in costume take water to the fields, from the sacred cistern on the south side of Acoma. It is very hard to get up or down the steps, through the sand. The girls go with men leaders, carrying the water on their heads. It is an honor to participate in that, and you can be asked over and over again."

"Also we visit the family graves with food in a pottery or china bowl. We take water there in a canteen, pour it where the head is so the spirit gets the water. Then I go to the other graves and pour the rest."

Recollecting pleasant times, Andrew continues, "Years ago they used to put tallow from animal fat in a pottery bowl with a cloth wick and burn it, like a candle. They also used dry cactus for torches. A lot of pottery was made, and still is, for use in the kiva and for giving at ceremonials and other times, but those bowls for the oil lamps were really nice. Each kiva has a wooden ladder with extra long ends. The smoke goes up the ladder, and you climb down through it. Discipline is very strong in our tribe. When we were younger the elders used to talk to us for hours and hours at a time. I am so glad for those talks."

I ask if there are roles for women, knowing that there are none in the inner workings of any pueblo. "Yes, of course," they tell me. "For ceremonies they make the food, grind corn, make pottery. They dance, too, at certain times." Women do not vote or hold any of the tribal offices, but one of Lucy's daughters says, "Women have a certain power—they give birth. Often their best role is to help at childbirths, to heal, to take away sadness. And it used to be the women who had the power to locate the enemy." I interject that the word "power" is difficult to explain, but that most Indians I have known seem to attach great importance to it, in both the secular and spiritual sense.

"We hardly talk about that. Power probably has different explanations in every tribe. Certain substances have power, like cornmeal and cattail pollen, and things have power, like the sun. Having a vision is powerful and gives power. Or you can inherit it. Power is sacred, no matter how you explain it. We are overwhelmed by these experiences, but we all strive to have them. Even in gathering clay you can have a profound experience. We Acoma are raised with great attention to this. Children are encouraged to dream and to tell their dreams the next day to the adults. We have a life of waking hours and a dream life."

During these discussions with Andrew, Dolores, Emma, and Lucy, singly or all together, I am constantly confronted with the responsibilities, demands, and hardships intrinsic to the life of these people. Where is the time to do pottery? All the raw materials for clay and painting have to be gathered and refined before the laborious processes of forming and firing. Many pots are needed for the kiva, for ceremonials, for gifts on special occasions. It is no wonder that only a few pots are made for sale every year, even by the most skilled artists.

The preparation of a feast, for example, may take many days. One Easter I arrived at Emma's house unknowingly at the time of the special ceremonial for this season. No Anglos are allowed to witness this ritual on the mesa, so I could not stay, nor could they show me the pottery processes we had discussed photographing.

On this occasion, however, Emma said, "Stay until tomorrow. We will be up at four o'clock to begin baking bread. You can watch." I once watched Santana and Adam Martinez make and bake forty loaves in their outdoor oven at San Ildefonso pueblo. (This is photographed in detail in my book on Maria Martinez.) Nevertheless, I was unprepared for the mountainous pillows of dough, rising up and cascading over the edges of several huge metal washtubs, in Emma's kitchen the next morning. The women were up before 4:00 A.M. and had started before I arrived. This dough would eventually yield about 270 round loaves of bread.

The kitchen is bustling with women and children. Rena, a guest from Jemez pueblo, is up to her elbows in a pan of dough, pushing her fists repeatedly into the erupting mass. Emma and her daughters are doing the same in other big pans. Someone is frying tortillas and making coffee. The men and boys are outside chopping juniper wood for the big adobe oven down by the road, where the bread will be baked.

Each batch of dough begins with fifty pounds of flour in a tub, spread out and sprinkled with a mixture of a half-pound of yeast and warm water. The children call the yeast froth on the flour "bubble bath" and giggle a lot. Two pounds of lard (bought or rendered) is added, and showered with several handfuls of the special local salt; then another two pounds of lard or so are worked into the dough in the pan. After the first rising, the dough is kneaded every thirty minutes, then left to rise again, covered with white sheets. Batches have been combined and now lap over the edges of the big pans.

At about ten o'clock, the first amount, perhaps fifty pounds, is laid out on the big table, with a sheet underneath; there are stacks of round soot-blackened pans nearby. "We don't know how many loaves we make, we never count. We just eat and give away," the women laugh. "Our bread always turns out good. Sometimes we sell it, too." Lucy cuts off a portion of dough from the big hump on the table, enough for one loaf, and kneads it. "We never measure size either," she says with a twinkle.

She flattens her chunk of dough on a board, picks it up in both hands, and shapes a fat round, smooth on top and folded under at the base. She flattens that and cuts it in three places, folds over the top, and spreads the three-cornered loaf out in one of the pans. Then she cuts another chunk to repeat the process. Around her, men and women are working, scrambling eggs with red hot chili and preparing a big breakfast. Everyone is chatting, happy about being together.

Each of the women has her own way to shape the round bread loaf. Emma makes about sixty mounds, kneaded and pinched, and arranges them, pinched side up, on a table and on boards on the floor. Then she works the loaves, rolling each one with a short wooden cylinder, turning and rolling it again, cutting it with a knife in three places on each side, larding the top, and flipping one side over the other into a half-circle. This is larded again and put in a pan, and the three fat sections are spread out from each other. This is the Lewis shape. "I don't make the dough too wet, but it takes longer to bake if it's too dry," she says, looking at the several hundred pans of dough all over the house.

Some of the women are making chili on Emma's gas range; later at Sky City they will make much more on the wood stove. Many thousands of green chilis from their summer garden have been canned or roasted (but not peeled) then frozen. Some of this chili is fried with the eggs, some put into the big stewpan of corn. Several sacks of peeled chilis go into the large pot where meat and onions have been browning. Water is added to the big pot of green chili, then two bulbs of garlic. In another large container, several pounds of powdered red chili have been added to the broth in which *pozole*—dried hominy—is stewing. The aromas of this kitchen are almost too rich to bear; I call them up out of memory when I am away from Acoma.

Tortilla dough uses vegetable shortening or lard and a little baking powder; perhaps two cups of flour make six tortillas. The dough is patted into portions the size of a baseball, then each one is rolled out, flipped, rolled again, and fried without oil in an iron pan. These are wrapped in a dishtowel and brought hot to the table; everyone pulls off pieces to eat with eggs and chili. I have noticed that it is possible for every meal to be nearly the same. The staples are chili of some kind and tortillas or adobe oven bread, with perhaps fruit or sweets added.

"Fry bread" is a treat and often made for festivals, to eat and to sell. The dough is a bit moister than that for tortillas. Women have different recipes for this, too: some say five cups of flour to a half cup of powdered milk; some say seven cups of flour plus "some lard cut in like biscuit dough." The Lewis women agree on three level teaspoons of baking powder for every two cups of flour, plus some local salt, and cold water. This mixture is vigorously kneaded, pulled, kneaded again, and formed into balls. Lard for deep-frying is melted and heated until it smokes. Dough rounds are rolled out, cut in quarters, spiked with fork holes, and dropped into the hot oil. They are turned once and drained quickly on paper. If the round is fried uncut, it can be the base on which to build an Acoma style open-faced sandwich, piled with lettuce, tomatoes, beans, and perhaps beef. *Sopaipillas* are made from the same recipe but without holes in the dough, so they puff up as they fry; these are eaten with powdered sugar or honey.

The large outdoor oven was built in 1955 of basalt, mortared and plastered with adobe. "It wasn't built in a day, you know," they all remark to me at one time or another. "You have to let it set up in between for days, layer by layer." The fire has been blazing inside for an hour and a half, and there is a lot of smoke and fire, some of which escapes from chinks in the old oven. Emma dumps a bucket of water on the ground nearby and makes a thick mud slurry with her shovel. Everyone pelts the cracks in the oven where the fire leaks through with handfuls of this mud. Lucy carries down the large oar-shaped paddle for putting in the bread.

Lee Mitchell, Emma's husband, shovels old ash away from the oven door and clears space for new coals and ash when they are swept out of the chamber. Lucy makes the longish walk back up to Emma's house, returns with a mop made of long strips of cloth tied to a handle, and lays it by the oven. The boys and girls have been carrying down the pans of dough on boards; the last trip is made with the remaining pans in the back of the truck and on the extended tailgate. The bread boards spread out on the ground about the oven.

Emma puts an old shirt on the end of a long stick, dunks it in water, and scatters the water over the pile of coals scraped out from the oven. When they bake in the winter, the girls say, they leave the coals hot on the ground to keep themselves warm; now it is spring, and they quench the coals. The oven is swabbed inside with the long-handled rag mop to clean away the ash. As fast as possible, the loaves are handed up and put on the flat end of the paddle; Emma thrusts them into the back of the oven, on the clay floor. The work has to be fast, or the oven will lose too much heat.

When the last loaf is in the oven, Lucy readies a large piece of canvas she has brought from the house in another trip up the road, and Emma claps a board over it to form a good seal on the oven opening. They pause to discuss how hot the oven is now, how hot it was, and how much of the firewood has been used; from that they determine not to cover the opening at the top. I tell Emma that she can use all this ash to make glaze for high-temperature firings, and a kiln from the oven by excavating a fire-box underneath. She grins and says she wouldn't know how.

Soon Lucy and her daughters stand at the opening and pull the board forward to peek. "Oh, it looks wonderful already . . . so nice and brown!" After about twelve minutes they remove the board keeping the mouth of the oven closed, "because the fire was so hot." Everything is working out perfectly, they agree. Lucy stands with her arms crossed, a half smile crinkling her strong face, eyes shining with the pleasure of a job well done.

The girls begin to tell me what could have gone wrong. If the oven is open too long and cools too much, or if they had too much water on the rag mop that cleans out the ashes, then they would have to start the fire again. "If you build the fire right you don't have to dip the mop more than once to wash down. We used to test it with cornmeal mush—throw it in there to see if it scorched immediately. Then you would dip the mop again and go over the floor lightly to cool it just a bit more. Now I just test it by how it feels on my arm or my face," explains the experienced Emma. "In the winter it usually snows, and it's a little harder then."

I marvel at their control of the process, which is akin to the difficulties of firing a wood-burning kiln. Even years of repeated practice cannot always guarantee success, because the factors of weather, wood, and dough are not constant. We all shake our heads and smile, excited by the aroma of hot bread.

After half an hour the canvas is removed. The bread remains another fifteen minutes, then is brought out with the same long paddle. The boys load the hot loaves on the truck and drive carefully up to the house. Some of the bread is eaten on the spot, everyone standing around the table piling on butter or dunking it in chili. The rest is wrapped in plastic and stored for the feast.

Although I will not be allowed to attend this feast, I was privileged to have been at last year's September ceremonial. I was asked to arrive on the night before, so we could all go up to the mesa together. Even at 6:00 P.M. it was pitch black when I arrived at Emma's house, after the flight from New York and the drive from Albuquerque.

The girls had packed the truck and the family's old Lincoln with water and food, and we began the twenty-mile trip through the valley to the foot of Sky City. The whole earth was silent. Stars burned large in the sky. The hills were now blue-violet and gray-black, punctuated by the huge sentinel rocks and the mesa. Automobile headlights were visible for miles, and from the top at Acoma tiny glimmers from candles and lanterns flickered and beckoned. It was all unreal.

At Lucy's house on the mesa the big metal cans of water were unloaded and stored outside, the cans in the kitchen filled, and the ice brought in—although it would not last long. The children and adults went their separate ways, the younger ones to fix mats for sleeping on the roof and in the big room. Everyone else went into the kitchen to talk and fix dinner.

Andrew had lit the house with kerosene and gas lanterns and hanging lamps. The light was subdued against the whitewashed walls; the shadows were deep and dark. There was a fire in the wood stove. We sat down at the big kitchen table, covered with a flower-patterned oilcloth, for the dinner of corn and chili and tortillas and bologna that we brought with us.

When supper was finished, the women silently took up the different tasks they have done so many times before. The turkey was made ready, to be cooked slowly all night in the wood stove. Fresh green chilis were dropped into an enormous stewpot, like a ten-gallon can, to be simmered with lamb. Red chili, from ground dried chili peppers, was set to brew in another pan, in broth with hominy. Burlap sacks of Indian corn, roasted in the husk in the adobe bread oven down below, were brought in still warm, for the next day. Someone observed that Acoma bread tasted like San Francisco sourdough, "but the texture is different."

Set on the table—permanently, I think—were shallow pottery bowls filled with the local salt, which was frequently added to the cook pots; everyone who passed would take a pinch. This coarse salt is brought from the salt flats southwest of the mesa, between Fence Lake and Red Hill, near the Arizona border. The Acoma people have always gone there to gather salt, I am told. The flavor is very different from commercial boxed salt, and I, too, cannot get enough of it. Used just as it comes from the flats, it has a mild, clean taste.

Seventeen of us found places to sleep in the house and on the roof. The next morning, we woke to the glow of dawn through the windows of the big open room; the men, who slept on the roof, were at their chores. Water was scarce, but there was enough for quick washing. The children were dressing themselves in ceremonial costume. Lucy, the earliest up, was already off to the plaza in her shell-pink outfit and green shawl, bedecked with turquoise jewelry. I remembered that turquoise and coral have special significance for these people.

The kitchen was bustling again. Breakfast that morning was part of the feast, which was to continue all day. To the chilis, tortillas, and turkey, fresh fruit was a welcome addition. All the families grow melons—"native melon," Andrew calls it—and the women had brought up baskets full. "They really are native because we grow them only from our own seeds. We don't eat market melons, so that no outside seeds can get in our planting," says one of Dolores' sons, who grows his own.

Emma's and Dolores's sons had roasted the white Indian corn in the bread oven for one day and were eager to taste it. Permission was granted, and corn in the husk was passed around for all to enjoy. It had a glorious sweet and tender flavor, unlike any corn I had ever tasted.

"You use an adobe oven, building coals from wood, or you can use charcoal brickettes," Andrew told me. "You put a bucket of water in there and close the oven fast so the corn steams. I can remember when my father used to put the head of a freshly butchered cow in the oven. The meat was so good!"

Lucy returned from the plaza and changed her dress and shawl again, this time to take food to the saint: a heavy basket full of choice oranges, apples, and melons. Emma and Dolores were waiting for the bells of the church to ring four times, for the Mass and then the procession. No one was going to the service, but they wanted to join the procession afterwards. In a few minutes Lucy returned, having left her offering to the saint. Some of her grandchildren scurried about to help her gather and carry the folding table and pottery she would take to the plaza, or nearby, to "set up." A few of them would sit with her, selling the pots, speaking only when spoken to.

Ivan and Rita Lewis arrived from Cochiti. Greetings are very subdued among the Acoma: a brief smile, a nod, a slight raise of the hand, or nothing at all. No form of touching or hugging is a part of their world, unless a demonstrative Anglo insists. Ivan is Lucy's oldest child, but his demeanor with the family is that of an agreeable stranger. He and Rita talked quietly, at their end of the table, eating chili and corn. No questions were asked of or by any of the family.

The "doings" at Cochiti pueblo were to last all the next week; Ivan was an official with special duties coming up and was glad for the chance to relax at Acoma. Everyone was waiting for the bells to ring, and when finally they did, we were all up and out of the house, walking toward the church for the end of the Mass.

The church had been painted inside in pink and white. The stations of the cross hung on the walls, something I had not seen before. Five rows of wooden pews were in front of the altar. The procession took the wooden image of Saint Stephen, patron of this pueblo, to its place of honor in an evergreen bower on the plaza. The saint was carried high, and the people followed, some singing or chanting, in a long winding line down the path between the ancient dwellings, around the edge of the mesa, and again through the buildings. Five visiting priests were last in the line. Dolores and others in Lucy's family joined the procession, as did I.

Andrew has often said that there should be no harm in observing the rites for both Indian and Christian gods. If one is good, two is better. That was his father's teaching, he explains.

Lucy herself did not join the procession. She had changed her clothing again, this time to ceremonial costume, and was wearing her black manta with the magnificent turquoise and silver manta pins from top to bottom, down the right side of her skirt. She stood in the plaza, by her table of pots. All the paths among the buildings were lined with colorful booths, many of them laden with "fry bread," homemade tamales of hand-ground cornmeal, nachos, and snow cones of precious ice and fruit syrups. Women were selling pottery, rain sashes, Indian-style shirts, moccasins, and buckskin leggings. People from other pueblos were allowed to sell their handcrafts. By this time a few tourists were visible in the milling crowd.

We returned to the house. The bustle of visitors going in and out in a sense belied the solemnity of the occasion. Andrew noted that this Catholic feast day for the village saint comes on the same day as the Acoma harvest dance—the corn dance. The Spanish fathers seem to have carefully chosen the saint for the village whose feast day was the same as the major annual Acoma ceremony. "Actually the feasts keep families and the pueblo close-knit," he said, "making the preparations and spending this kind of time together. Nearly everyone comes, especially to the dances this afternoon."

Emma and Dolores stood at the stove, ladling chili, seeing to it that the visitors had bowls and spoons at the table and plenty of tortillas and adobe oven bread. There were prune-stuffed squares of sweet tortilla dough on the table, piled high on a tray, and cookies. (At Acoma every sweet made with tortilla dough seems to be called "pie," no matter what the shape.) The women took turns at cooking, laying the table for every shift of diners, and hovering over guests. Some friends of the family dropped by to help. There were very few Anglos on the plaza, but any visitor who walked in the door of any house on the pueblo that day, even if he or she was a complete stranger, would be fed.

Without preamble the extended family rose and left the house, bound for the open plaza and the ceremonial dances. The site was a small oblong in the center of the pueblo, with a raised adobe terrace for seating. At the north end was the sanctuary for the saint, under green boughs symbolizing everlasting life. The spectators are closer to the dancers here than at most ceremonials (except perhaps in the Hopi pueblos), because the space is hemmed in by buildings. When the dancers and drummers are almost on top of you, involvement in the rhythm of the dance is profound; the earth actually seems to shake in resonance to the beat.

The infectious pounding of the drum, unvarying to the Anglo ear but actually filled with frequent and subtle change of rhythm...the male singers...the children imitating their elders in step and gesture...rattles...moccasined feet...the hypnotic power of sounds and movements repeated again and...the intense expressions on the painted faces of the dancers, all different yet all alike...dancing for supplication, dancing for well being...the riot of colors...strange greens and pinks and yellows, satin ribbons, calico prints, paisley back-aprons, lace and velvet trims...necklace and bracelets and cuffs of turquoise and coral and tiny shell beads...leg bells and anklets of bells...feathers...the chant rising and falling...an awesome experience, the Indian dance.

The dances and the feast ended at sundown. Lucy had sold all the pottery she had on the table, perhaps eight pieces. A group of more distant relatives gathered in the house, around the table still covered with food. It was dark again, peaceful and quiet, but in our heads the drums still beat, the kaleidoscope of colors still whirled and tumbled.

LUCY HAS NINE CHILDREN LIVING: two sons and seven daughters. She has forty-five grandchildren, forty-six great-grand-children, and "some" great-great-grandchildren at the last count. The family is con-tinually growing. She knows each one of them by name and often sees those who live nearby. All the young children call her Nana and hang on to her skirts, waiting for the pennies she may award or the more serious presents of pottery at ceremonial times.

Lucy and her husband Toribio lived at Sky City when their first five children were born. As times changed and living on the mesa became more difficult, Toribio took his family down to a small house on the ridge at McCartys village, near the highway and nearer the crops. Families began moving down from the mesa in the 1920s, because many of Lucy's generation who had not gone to school wanted the next generation to have an education.

Toribio, who died in 1966, to some degree had an influence on all the children—more so on the older ones, especially the sons. Lucy's fame as a potter did not arrive until the 1950s; the older children grew up without that awareness. The younger ones had special advantages because of her renown, but Lucy's cooking, canning, and gardening were things of the past by this time, and they missed out on that. Most important, perhaps, were the differences that resulted as the children faced the problems of the day, which, for American Indians, include of domestic policy changes in Washington that the Anglo world is largely unaware of.

There were great differences in educational opportunity from the time of the oldest of Lucy's children to the youngest. The way of life changed appreciably in that twenty-eight year span in which her children were born. As new values emerged, there were revisions in the government school policies, especially in regard to the use of the Keresan language. Lucy's first children were sent to Indian boarding schools, for the most part, and the last to public schools. Ivan, the oldest, says there was no opportunity for him to go to college, although he wanted to do so; a few of his younger siblings were able to find a way. One of the youngest joined the Peace Corps.

All but two of the children live now on Indian reservations, and those two return often. Some are more immersed than others in Indian ritual practice, but all follow the traditional path in their own ways. Children no longer, they are fully-formed personalities in their own right; what links them together is their common bond with Lucy.

IVAN

Ivan Lewis, the first born, remembers: "I grew up on the mesa and used to dance in bare feet with a hole in my breeches. Some of my younger brothers and sisters didn't have that chance, although they came up to the pueblo for feasts after they were nine or ten. I had the best of it, born first. At that time you could stay with one family, then another. Until I was about five or six, everyone wanted me. When I went to day school at McCartys, I stayed with my father's people. My father was raising cows and farming, and I helped, especially in the summer."

When he was nine or ten, Ivan was sent to Santa Fe Indian School, which was for boarding students. It was too far from Acoma for him to come home more than once a year. Looking back at sixty-four, he does not see that as a hardship, but he finds it amazing that distances seemed so much greater in wagons than in cars. At the Indian School the children had to wear uniforms and drill, but Ivan thought it was a good school. He did well and became a track star.

"I got to be a runner through my uncle," he says. "My uncle knew Jim Thorpe. We used to chase that uncle around the pueblo, when he was home, and he would tell us how Jim did it. That got me interested in running. I ran all the time and I ran for the high school and for the marines when I got there." It is likely that Ivan would have been part of the U.S. Olympic team if there had been no war.

"Even in high school I was starting to be on my own, starting to think what I wanted to be. When I was thirteen or so the government offered to sell us registered bulls. Three of us cattlemen decided to buy bulls together and have registered cattle. The government took some old cows for part of the payment and the next year some calves for more. It cost $1200 for each bull; three of us bought one. In three years we had a good herd; the improvement really showed up. People used to wonder why we got so much more at the cattle sales. When they discovered what a difference it made, they formed a cattle association and chose my dad to be the head, so it helped everybody in Acoma."

As long as Ivan can remember, Lucy was a potter—as were his grandmother Lola and his aunt Helice, Lola's sister. "She was just a little lady, not more than a hundred pounds, and not five foot tall, but she made huge pots you can see now at the Laboratory of Anthropology in Santa Fe. The ladies used to work together, including Lucy, and I used to go with her to sell ashtrays for fifteen cents at the train station."

"If grandmother Lola in Grants ran short on pots, she would send the word to Lucy, and I would get in the covered wagon—though I was pretty small—and hitch the team. It took all day to go that seventeen miles, to take the pots to town. The money from the pottery was pooled. It went to buy groceries to keep the entire family—cousins, aunts, everyone."

"How did your mother get famous?" I ask. Ivan responds that somewhere along Lucy started working with the fine-line designs and the corrugated pottery she saw on the old shards. Then people noticed, and later she won a blue ribbon at the Gallup Intertribal. "My wife, Rita, and I took a lot of blue ribbons for our work, too, but now we don't enter anymore. We think it is getting too commercial, and many of the pieces aren't traditionally made—even if they say so. The standards aren't high now, we think. We just want to make what our grandfathers made."

"Rita and I graduated from Santa Fe Indian School and would have liked to go on, but we couldn't. We worked all our lives for our children to go to school. Indians, I don't care where they are—their children are always there. If any of them need anything, until the end of their days, they will get it; it's not like Anglos do." Ivan talks about the house he and Rita built in the new development at Cochiti, twelve years ago: "It was part of the government housing project except that twenty-five of us decided to come out here away from the plaza. We all helped each other build; we did everything together. Now the young people get contractors for the new houses."

Ivan and Rita recall that they sold a lot of chili and bread to support their children while they were going to school away from the pueblo. They are proud that all of them are doing meaningful, useful work: Ronald is employed at the Public Health Hospital in Santa Fe; Alvin is an engineer in Alaska; Patricia teaches at the Santo Domingo pueblo elementary school; Joseph is an electronic engineer at the Sandia atomic energy laboratory; and James works with an Indian organization that serves all the pueblos.

These Lewises have lived on Rita's pueblo for forty years, since Ivan returned from the war. He has been lieutenant governor of Cochiti and war chief and now is a lifetime councilman. He no longer has any affiliation with Acoma pueblo, where he was born. Women are not allowed to vote at Cochiti—or at any pueblo that Rita knows of—but she says she does not mind, "those men can take charge."

"Once you have the Indian tongue," Ivan remarks, you will always have it no matter where you go. Then you can never lose your Indian nature. You can bend children when they're still young, like a young limb. When they get too big you can't bend them, so you best do it early, like the willow. There's a lot of ways the old folks have of making you understand."

"Our great-grandfathers knew; they knew much. Mine, he was older than 110. They knew these days were coming. He used to tell me: 'Grandson, don't smoke or you'll be weak. Don't eat too much. Don't drink water. One of these days you boys are going to war.' I found out my great-grandfather was right when I got to World War II. Years ago he said that one of these days there would be fire through the air. We think that's jet propulsion. He said to keep in mind four things: there will be four great wars; the third one hasn't happened yet, and the fourth one will burn everything. I don't know how those old men knew! They even talked about a time to come when young ones wouldn't mind their elders. Ever since the moon landing I notice things have changed. The growing season is shorter. The weather is different."

Ivan is finished talking to me. He and Rita are well known as potters in the tradition of the old clay figures from the 1700s, the "storyteller" dolls that Helen Cordoro has popularized. Now they have work to do. Rita brings out the figures for a creche, part of a large commission from a bank for use as a window display. She needs to paint the polished white surface with black lines, to add faces and details.

Ivan sets up a folding table in the living room and starts the kneading process to bring his iron-red clay into pliability. His big hands squeeze the fat wads of clay into coils, for the legs, body, and head of the doll, which he puts together flat on a board. From a cupboard he brings out photographs and Xerox copies he has made from books in the museum. "According to the research I've done, these figures are how the old folks pictured the tourists, the old cowboys—I make cowboys—and the priests. The Indian Arts Research Center in Santa Fe has a good collection of the old figures. Rita's mother was a storyteller doll maker; now she makes them."

The Cochiti clay is full of iron oxide and it fires very dark, even at dung temperature. The white slip applied over it for the polished coating comes from Santo Domingo pueblo and fires a warm, mellow gray from the dark clay underneath. The slip is so thick it takes all day to cover one figure, Rita says. "It has to dry between coats; then, when there's enough, you rub it to shine. I do many at a time. When they were building the dam Ivan worked on, he remembers seeing a pure white clay in the earth where the steam shovel made the hole, but it was immediately covered up. That means that somewhere at Cochiti we should be able to find clay of our own for the white slip, so we wouldn't have to buy from another pueblo, but we never have seen it again."

Ivan, now retired, worked on the construction of the big government dam that bisected this pueblo. "Most of our red clay was submerged behind that dam," he complains. "Right now it's even hard to find manure. We don't have many cows, and a lot of ladies are making pottery and doing their own firing; we all need cow chips. I have told Emma's and Dolores' boys I'd pay for anything they can find me at Acoma."

The black pigment Rita uses for drawing the features and details on the figures is wild "mountain spinach," also called Rocky Mountain bee plant by some and known as *guaco* to the Pueblo people. (This is also discussed in my book on Maria Martinez.) Rita uses only the leaves, because the stalks are harsh, boiling them in a caldron outside for two days to reduce the pigment to a paste, then spreads this one-half-inch thick on cornhusks. She maintains that if it sits for a few years, it gets better—adheres better and even fires blacker. The last batch she made six years ago. When she needs it, she softens a cake of *guaco* with water and waits for it to reach the right consistency for painting. Only vegetable pigments are used at Cochiti, not mineral.

Ivan and Rita fire their storytellers and cowboys one at a time on a metal grate off the ground. They burn wood under it into coals, then place one figure on the grate, covering this with a wire hood. Dry dung patties are built up over the wire, the small chips closest because they will get hottest and hold the heat, and the bigger chips on top. If there is wind, they use a metal shield. When Ivan can see red heat inside, and the cow chips outside are reduced to white ash, he takes the figure out with long tongs and inserts another. It takes all day to fire a group.

Outside, next to where they build the dung kiln, are two adobe bread ovens. Rita says they go to the hills for the wood, and their boys come to help chop it. "We use a lot of wood for baking in these two ovens. We roast corn on top of hot coals and lava rock. You leave it in all night with the door mudded up and put water in through the hole in the top for steam, so the corn won't burn. I make pies in these ovens—pumpkin, prune, any kind—and sweet bread, as well as adobe oven bread for the feasts."

Some of the Ivan Lewis children and daughters-in-law are also learning to make the dolls, because they want to know how to pass on the skills and traditional ways of working unique to this pueblo. The children and the eleven grandchildren are all proud of Ivan and Rita when they see their clay figures in the gallery windows on the plaza in Santa Fe.

Emma

Emma, Lucy's fifth child—the fourth daughter—was born at old Acoma in 1931. She lives now with her Navajo husband, Lee Mitchell, and their children and grandchildren in a house on the hillside in the village below the mesa. On the road below, near the highway, is the adobe Toribio built, where the family lived part-time when Emma was growing up. Today the women use that house to store cow chips for the pottery-firings. Further up the path is another adobe house occupied now by Lucy's youngest daughter. Past the corn and melon field, toward the hills, is Emma's house.

"All I remember about growing up is feeding the pigs and the chickens. That was my chore for years," she says. Emma attended the pueblo day school and the public school in Albuquerque, then was sent to Fort Wingate for the seventh and eighth grades. She went on to the Santa Fe Indian School, where she graduated from high school. "Lucy was always making pottery," she recalls, "except in winter she crocheted and did embroidery. She always made the pottery by herself, never asked for help. We played with the clay."

Emma entered Haskell Institute, the Indian school in Lawrence, Kansas, for two years of junior college, then took a job as domitory supervisor at the Fort Sill Indian School in Oklahoma. There she met her husband and stayed while Lee was in the marines. When their first child was born, Emma and Lee returned to Acoma to settle down. "I know other tribes and Indians from other pueblos," she says, "because I was in so many schools. When we were in school we were all punished if we talked our own languages. Now they *want* us to talk our language; they teach it at the day school."

"I've always been on my own," she continues. "I began making pottery after I had the children, and I first took small pots to the Flagstaff Fourth of July Indian Pow-Wow in 1966. Can I be making pottery seventeen years? Well, from the beginning Lucy would help me—not much, but she did help. She'd talk to me about my shapes and she showed me how to paint. She'd paint and I'd watch, and that's how I learned the designs. Now I work out my own."

Emma makes pottery between her household chores. She keeps the pots in progress on a chest in the kitchen, where they can be easily moved to the table for more work. Her low painting table, with its jeweler's lamp and metate for grinding mineral pigments, is near the kitchen sink. After grinding and screening her clay outside, she mixes it with water for plasticity on the kitchen floor, on her hands and knees or with her feet. Children are around her most of the time.

"After Lucy got recognized she told us to get started making pottery. She was getting more money from the traders than when she sold on the highway. Dolores and I have always lived nearby. Dolores hardly left the reservation, and since Oklahoma we have always been here. We're the closest to our mother; we take care of her—she lives with Dolores and her children—and one of us takes her everywhere she wants to go."

Emma finds it hard to remember how it was when she was a litttle girl, because the days are almost all the same in a pueblo village; nothing changes much. She gets up from the table and begins preparations for the traditional meal she has promised me. Her six children—Leland, Monty, Valerie, Monica, Seth, and Claudia—and eleven grandchildren are on hand for most mealtimes. "I'm a grandmother left and right!" Emma says, and starts the tortillas.

Deftly she pats the dough into lumps the size of baseballs and lines them up on the counter. Then she pulls each one out with her fingers into a thick, flat circle, and rolls it thinner and larger with a thin rolling pin. She browns the tortillas on a hot iron grill, flipping each one when brown spots appear. The hot rounds are piled in a tea towel to keep warm until the rest of the food is ready.

Emma decides to make an Indian pudding the way Lucy taught her. Wheat soaked in water until it sprouts is thoroughly dried and then ground on a metate. Sugar is browned with a little water in a saucepan, and to this is added white flour and the ground malted wheat. "There's no measurements; we just guess," is Emma's answer to my unuttered question. (I have watched the Lewis women making many different foods often enough to know that none of them uses anything more exact than fingers or a cupped palm to measure ingredients.) Usually this pudding is baked in an outdoor adobe oven, in a galvanized bucket lined with cornhusks, for about an hour.

"This is what we always eat at Easter time," Emma explains, "but now, what a treat! We make Easter cake from the same recipe, only it's stiffer. The batter is more like dough, enough so you can spread it in a circle on a cornhusk. You bake those in the oven outdoors, take them out, and put two together with the cornhusks on the outside, so the cakes won't dry out. The Hopis make good pudding, too, but from roasted and ground corn, not wheat." Everyone says that Emma is one of the best cooks in the family, but my own experience tells me they are all good, the men too. Emma and I joke about that for a moment.

Emma's green chili stew is made today with ground beef browned with onions, plenty of water for the broth, and lots of green chilis from the garden—roasted last summer and frozen in plastic bags, to be thawed and peeled as they are needed, all winter. To the green chilis in the big container, Emma adds a pan of corn, then makes the ever-present sweet punch in a large plastic pitcher, and summons the family. Children spill out into other rooms with their plates because not everyone can fit at the kitchen table.

The tortillas go in the middle of the table; a bowl and spoon are at each place. Everyone reaches to tear off a portion of tortilla to butter or to fold over a center of the fiery chili. The cold drink is a necessity for the Anglo palate, but merely a refreshment to these people, for whom heavily spiced chili dishes are a part of everyday life. The pudding is in a large bowl on the table; some eat it with the chili and others save it for last. What remains is set aside to take to Lucy when Emma visits, because it is her mother's favorite sweet.

Emma has been pensive during the meal, thinking about her childhood. "We used to get up early, before the sun rises, so we could go out with our dad to hoe weeds in the garden. Sometimes we took the wagon because the farm was near our father's sister's house. I was about ten years old. We grew onions, carrots, cabbage, beets, corn, green beans, turnips, tomatoes, chilis, pumpkins, and melons. I don't know what we did with all that; I don't think we could can it all for winter. There were fruit trees, and we dried the fruit too. I guess we gave away what we couldn't use to other families that didn't garden."

"When I was going to the day school there was no radio, no electricity, only kerosene lamps down here. We used to sit around the wood stove, and my dad would tell us stories. Such long stories they were. You have to sit up a long time—hours—to hear those old stories. Meantime my mom would be parching corn. She had this cast-iron pot with three legs. She used that fine sand that comes from down in the arroyo. When the sand got hot in the pot she'd put the corn in and stir with a cedar stick."

"She had to sift the sand out, and you never did see a speck of sand on that corn; I don't know how. Then she would take salt and brush it on the corn with a corncob. She would roast piñons, too, in the same pot. And we would eat this while we were listening to the stories. If Lucy had apples, she'd bring a bowl of those, and they were good with the hot corn. I'm sure all that good food helped us sit through the stories."

"I wish I remembered how they went, but they were so long. Of course I think they became part of us, helped us, even if we don't remember exactly. It was just me and one or two of the other children maybe. As our father was telling the stories, there was a word, "*eh heh*," we had to say at the end of every segment. I guess maybe that was what kept us awake."

"Lucy told me her grandfather used to tell the same stories when she was little, up on the mesa. But now she has forgotten them. She says there are songs coming from these stories, for everything on earth, but that she is so old now that she can't remember." I do not express the thought, but I am thinking that this is one time when writing would have been an asset. I do not discuss it, because the Acoma do not write things down, even for their own posterity.

DOLORES

"I was born at McCartys in 1938, in the old house," she says, "the first house we had below the mesa. Somewhere along the line that house just disappeared, but I remember how it looked." Dolores is Lucy's seventh child—the fifth daughter. She attended the pueblo day school until the fourth grade, then went to Albuquerque and stayed with an older sister to attend public school. "None of us children were in school together," she recalls. "Not that we were so far apart; we were just sent to different places, all scattered."

In Albuquerque, I learned English at ten or eleven in the public school. It was a struggle, because I had never spoken it. But my mother and father didn't want the last of the three children to go to the Bureau of Indian Affairs schools, where they wouldn't let us use our own language. Indian schools are government schools and don't cost money. Most of us were sent away to one of them at one time or another, but no one liked it much. I remember our father talked about being sent to St. Catherine's school in Santa Fe for a while. It must have been free then, but it costs money now. Our father ran away and he didn't go back."

I sent my children to public school; so did Emma. Laguna and Acoma have a high school together at Laguna reservation, and some youngsters go to Catholic boarding school, but ours go to Grants public school together with all kinds of kids. I used to be afraid to talk English in front of Anglos. I didn't want my children to be like that."

Dolores muses, "When we were growing up we only spoke Acoma at home. In public school we learned our English from the same books the Anglos learned from, only they already spoke English. That was very difficult. At Indian schools they had a lot of different punishments if you spoke your own language. Once a week at day school on the pueblo a nun came to teach us catechism; we had to learn that in English even if we didn't know what it meant. Today our children are bilingual when they're little, but some don't know much Indian later on."

It was hard in Albuquerque. Because her older sister had her own children to care for, Dolores returned home to finish high school in Grants. This was when Lucy was quite ill and everyone was helping to look after her. Lucy has lived with Dolores since that time, and Dolores feels more fortunate than her sisters and brothers for that reason. "I say I'm the luckiest one in the family that I have my mother. Somebody chose me to be with her."

Dolores's eldest son, Adam, is quite eloquent about his grandmother. "It makes me feel good every time I see or think about my grandmother. From my earliest memories of childhood, she was always there, in person or in the potteries she was making that were in various stages of construction, when she wasn't around. When I was growing up, her pottery is the one thing that really stands out. She would go to shows off the reservation. When she would get home we would see news clippings and awards about her pottery that made me feel proud. People recognized her talent and her continuation of a tradition. Tradition is very important in our family, in the way we compare it with the Anglo world around us. In my grandmother's pottery I think about the great cultures here in New Mexico, who we maybe are descended from, and how she has kept the tradition of pottery making alive. It makes me feel good to know that I know where I come from."

"Emma has more children than I do, and many grandchildren," Dolores states, by way of explaining that Lucy could not live with Emma. "Children go to the mother of the mother. Technically, Emma has responsibility for the children of her two daughters. A son is supposed to move to his wife's house, but it's not always that way. Emma's sons and their families live with Emma. At Acoma you give up your community rights if you go to another pueblo." Dolores laments that her one grandchild is her son's child, so the boy "belongs" to his maternal grandmother. The children are members of the mother's clan. All agree that the one good thing about having girls is that the clan expands. "At San Ildefonso, children go to the father's clan," Dolores adds as an aside.

"So many families have trouble with children now. I guess it's like that everywhere. But we live so close, that makes it hard. Some families, if they don't have children, they raise someone else's; complications start there, too. But even if it makes problems, we still do that. There is always someone who wants to take babies, and we think girls should have babies, married or not."

Dolores lives in a tract of stucco houses built by the government, on paved streets near the Acoma day school. Her three boys, Adam, Chris, and Merle, and her daughter Kathleen live with her. Grandmother Lucy is up at seven or eight, working on her pottery at the kitchen table. When I am there, the family sits around this table to eat breakfast and visit, among the pots.

"I used to help myself to the clay," Dolores replies when I ask her if she worked in pottery as a young girl. "Lucy said not to waste clay, so I started with small pieces. I made pottery on weekends when I was in school. I'm sorry I didn't pay attention to my own Kathleen making pottery. She started, but I didn't help, and the clay dried out. But I think she will start again. One day Merle was sitting here, watching me painting. He said he wanted to paint, but his hands would shake. He's afraid. I told him it takes time to learn to hold steady, lots of time. Our children don't seem to want to take that time yet, but they watch Lucy; after all, she's right here working."

My questions make Dolores want to remember more of her childhood, and she relaxes her usual guarded reserve. "When I was in high school," she says, "most Indians were rebelling against traditional ways, wanted nothing to do with them. The government schools had done a good job of getting us not to use our own language and making us more like Anglos. But when the Alcatraz sit-in came, it gave us a new feeling, sort of a pleasure in finding our old ways. I think there is a revival—maybe not with all Indians—to learn more about our rituals again and be prouder of our people."

This is the most positive commitment to the future any member of this family has made to me, and I tell Dolores how pleased I am to hear that dedication in her voice. Dolores' sons have joined us, and they stand respectfully in the room, listening. All three have graduated from public high school but show little interest in the world outside Acoma. They tend small vegetable gardens, grow wheat and corn, work on the truck, and run errands for other members of the family. Whenever I am there I talk to them about college or trade school, about broader horizons that might include economic goals as well. But getting more education would mean partaking in more of the Anglo world, and of that there is an unspoken fear.

Dolores and I have talked several times of this problem. We have discussed what our friend Fred Kabotie did for his people at Hopi by building the Indian Arts and Crafts Center—with the help, finally, of the United States government. A training program in silversmithing and sales is available there for the young people of his pueblo. Of course this is only part of the answer, but we agree that it has done something important for the Hopi.

"I wish we had talked more to our father or our grandparents," Dolores continues, "but we didn't know to, I guess. Now our youngsters want to know more again, at least half of them here at the pueblo. It would take a whole lifetime to gather all that unless you kept at it all the time, but we're trying. Nothing is ever written down; you learn from each other or the elders or your family. I don't know it all—women can't," she shakes her head. "Our children participate, when it comes their turn, in ceremonials." She has revealed more of herself in these few minutes than it is her people's custom to do, and she turns again to the stove.

This morning she has made a new kind of chili she wants me to try; there is a big "doing" at the old place, and they will all go there tonight, which explains the size of the stewpot she is using. Large, flat chunks of beef jerky are browned in butter with onions, filling the room with an irresitible aroma. Dolores moves into the sitting room, sets her son Merle up at a small stool, fixes a hand-cranked grinding machine to the edge, and brings him a bucket of dried corn. Merle begins to turn the blade, grinding the meal into a flat pan; he checks with his mother about the coarseness and adjusts it to her specifications.

To the large container on the stove Dolores has added the browned jerky and onions, making a broth with water and very hot dried red chili powder, letting it simmer while she fries fresh tortillas in an iron skillet without fat. Merle brings several pans of the coarse cornmeal to the kitchen, one after the other, and dumps them into the steaming mixture. Instantly the stew thickens to the consistency of a mush. This will be eaten all day on pieces of fresh tortilla.

We are talking this morning with Lucy about her reaction to the photography and note-taking for the book. Dolores is not certain Lucy understands how a book about her will turn out, and once more my book on Maria Martinez is brought out. Lucy thumbs through it at the table. She talks in Keresan to Dolores, who translates to me that Lucy has always hoped for her own book, so she allows the photographing. But she does not understand why I have to write so much. Then she laughs and says she guesses it cannot write itself. She is so impressed with how Maria looks in the pictures that she goes off to change her dress.

BELLE

Belle is the next-to-last of Lucy's children and has gone farther than most into the Anglo world, but she remains steadfast to her own heritage. She lives with her husband and their three children at Laguna pueblo, about twenty miles east of Acoma.

The whitewashed church of Laguna and the surrounding adobes on the hill are visible from the highway, and there is a historical marker by the road. Laguna is the only one of the nineteen pueblos that observant tourists can glimpse without driving closer.

Belle attended McCartys day school, Santa Fe Indian School, finished high school at the public school in Grants, and went to Fort Lewis College in Durango, Colorado. In 1966 she joined the Peace Corps and was sent to Jamaica to train teachers. She herself has taught elementary school on the Laguna reservation for twelve years and is now on leave with a new baby. "Our children have only Indian names, not Anglo," she tells me. "Shayai is nine, Payadyamu is five, and Hiitsi, nine months."

Her husband, Stanley Lucero, spends most of his time as a tribal councilman, seeing to the needs of the pueblo as it strives simultaneously to keep its Indian ways and interact with the Anglo world. The reservation is rich in uranium and copper; income from these sources is used for communal needs, pueblo improvements, and scholarships for the young people—all tribal council business. A tall, handsome man whose remarkable braids have fourteen years of growth, Stan is an accomplished draftsman and artist. He publishes an Indian design calendar and note papers and has just begun a cabinet-making shop.

"Our father always farmed," says Belle. "Once a year we butchered a cow and canned or jerked it. We dried the bones to use in stew later in the winter. We blew up intestines, hung and then cooked that, also the udder, and we canned some intestines. People don't do this so much any more, but we still make jerky. Sometimes Lucy would hoe weeds with our dad after the planting; it was something they could do together."

Belle remembers her mother busy from morning to night, not just with pottery, but with many different things. "She used to crochet, especially, and she was telling me just the other day how sad she is that she doesn't have time for that any more. I remember Lucy was always making pottery, too. As a young child I went with her to sell the wares. I think there is a picture of me somewhere in a wheelbarrow by the pots," she continues. It is a memory that most of Lucy's children share.

"We used to play along the irrigation ditch near the house, before the freeway came. We made pots from the clay there and fired them with horse manure, but we couldn't fire them hot enough to keep!" We laugh over the image of the children imitating their elders without much sense of the skill required for a dung firing.

"Lucy didn't want help," Belle continues. "I guess she always wanted to do everything herself—gather the clay, grind it, wash it, mix it, and make the pots herself. The polishing and decorating, too." It may be that working by herself in the early years is what kept Lucy apart from the indigenous potting community and kept her work singing with grace and individuality.

Belle and I talk a bit about that. Lucy's children were not coopted to help when they were younger, nor were they encouraged to make pots on their own, as many children of potters were in other pueblos—or even at Acoma itself. Lucy was an example, however, and today all of her children do make some pottery, even if only for ceremonial use. The ones who sell their work are diverse in their shapes and styles, but the essential skill and approaches are noticeably similar.

"I am glad my brothers and sisters are carrying on with the traditional pottery,"

Belle says. "I never had time, what with teaching and raising my children, to keep mine going, but I want to make more. I would like to have my mom teach me how to mix the clay and the pigment, because those parts are so difficult. I hope I will have time to learn."

ANDREW

Lucy's fourth child—her second son—is adamant about the value of his early training. Andrew maintains that the lessons he received from his father, from other close relatives, and from elders at the pueblo, have been his lifelong guides.

"My father taught me how to ride, how to take care of the house, how to chop wood," he says, "and when we were out in the hills together for long weeks, he taught me many things about how to survive. If I did something wrong, one of my parents would come over and tell me what I should do. Our dad's philosophy was 'don't argue back.'"

"Lucy's grandfather had sheep and goats and he traded them for cows. Cows don't have to be watched all the time. I remember in high school having a girl friend who told me her family had acquired our sheep. That great-grandfather gave me my Indian name, Kiowai, which means 'winnowing wheat.' He was pretty old when I was a little boy, so he wanted me to have his own name."

"Dad taught me how to farm, how to drive a team of horses, how to hold a plow and plant and irrigate. He taught me when corn starts to ripen and when to pick in the fall. We didn't waste anything; we cut the stalks for animal feed during winter. I don't remember much about the Depression, but with those cattle we always had food; the family didn't starve." Born in 1927, Andrew was too young to remember, but he knows that his father was a tribal officer, the head *fiscale*, at about that time.

"Every day I worked hard with my dad," he continues, "and if I was lucky, my friends and I could go swimming or fishing one day a week or so. I still think about those days, because they were fun. We could do anything we wanted—play hide and seek in the hills, catch fish with our hands, pick and eat peaches and melons when they were ripe."

"Kids are growing up today in a different world. We sit down, talk to them; they walk out the door and forget. They participate in ceremonies only once, just for curiosity. If they don't take more time with it, we will lose our culture. Let's keep trying, I say. We try to encourage them to learn our language, because it's almost necessary to the rituals. Some are coming back to it. Of course our family's fortunate—we have Lucy."

"I was about five or six when I was playing around McCartys village. Aunt Helice Vallo would ask me to take her up to Acoma, and we'd go in the wagon. She used to make those real big pots; they were all good. I feel she used to favor me. She'd grind down some red chill on a stone and make a fresh tortilla and spread butter on it and put that ground red chili on top like jam. Then she'd say, 'Here, Andrew.' If she was grinding meat, she'd say, 'Here, Andrew,' and give me a bit of it. So maybe some of her pot-making rubbed off on me and helps me make pottery today."

"When I started to notice what my mother was doing, my older sisters were all away at school, so my younger sisters and I helped dad gather the cow dung in the wagon. Lucy looked for pot shards and pounded them herself and mixed them with the fresh clay. My dad would get the colors from a dry creek bed when he came in from farming. Lucy ground the rock or the pigment to see if it was the right color. She used only what was familiar; she didn't want to experiment—still doesn't. We younger ones are more willing. It was much later before she exhibited. Over in Paris somewhere she has a pot; one of the Acoma boys went there and happened on it. Also at the Smithsonian I guess there are some of hers."

This particular evening we are in the old house on the mesa. We need to drive down to the small store at Paguate for food; there is no refrigeration at Sky City, and such trips are necessary from time to time. Andrew has no car of his own and welcomes my offer of transportation. Clouds alternately cover and reveal a full moon; the yellow ochre earth is blue-gray now, lighter and darker as the vegetation changes. Occasionally a light flashes above the mountains: a falling star. All is quiet—totally quiet. Where else in this country is it so still? There is not a sound on the mesa as we leave the house, lanterns burning to welcome us back. I know that at dawn this quiet will be broken by the soft chirping of the wrens, and nothing else.

On the way to Paguate, Andrew reminisces: "I used to sing at the pow-wows, and then when I couldn't carry that high tone I just danced. Pow-wows aren't ceremonials, just demonstrations. When I first began going to them I won a third prize wearing the big Buffalo mask with horns and hair that came down over my eyes. I put my own paint make-up on myself, but at first I didn't know how, and sometimes I looked like the Lone Ranger. I just watched other men and tried to do like they did."

As we drive in the direction of Mount Taylor, he notes that it is time to begin laying in the wood for winter. It will take many loads. I recall that up at Acoma there is an indentation in the rocks about twenty feet wide, by Lucy's house, where several rows of logs are already stacked. Andrew will go to the hills, miles away, searching for downed trees—the dryest for burning. He says that Acoma people have been bringing wood back from this place so long that it is harder and harder to find trees. "If a man sees you with a log," he laughs, "he will always ask where you got it, but you just wave your hands around so he can't possibly tell which direction you mean!"

Andrew sees great differences in the two cultures, in the way each does things. He believes that having both Indian and Anglo experiences confuses the young people, that it would be better for them if they were educated on the pueblo and never left it, but he understands that this is impossible. "The young people," he continues, shaking his head, "don't know who they are or where they are going. We have to figure out how to help them."

The Bureau of Indian Affairs schools that prevented the people of his generation from speaking their own language now try to get instructors to teach bilingually. I observe that this single deprivation has left almost as much resentment against the Anglo in their hearts as the atrocities of the Spaniards, or the land grab of later years, but Andrew has a milder view. "I really liked school at the pueblo," he says. "When I was in second grade, at the end of the year they gave a prize. I got it for not missing one day all year. I got a toy airplane with a string attached—swing it around over your head and the propeller would turn. We walked to school thirty minutes or an hour, came home for lunch, and walked back. Today it's too easy."

Andrew was sent to the Indian School at Fort Wingate. There he received his first instruction in blacksmithing and woodworking and decided he would like to become an artist. He was brought home to Acoma when World War II broke out and finished high school in Grants. "From the old folks we heard stories of the First World War. They said that wars among Indians were different. My father told us the stories he learned from his father. They predicted that there'd be another war, that people would travel faster, in boxes—I guess they meant cars—and that there would be iron roads—railroads; how could they know? They predicted a rain of flames; we think that meant bombs. They told the boys a long time ago to learn to do without water and not to eat but just enough, because there would come a time when they would need this learning. The boys who went in the service in the first war, when they came back they said those old timers were right. The discipline I learned from my dad helped me, too, when I went in the army."

Andrew would like a computer, he thinks, to record the words and music of the ritual songs. He learned them from an old man, gone now, and he is training two younger men. He knows sixty songs that go on all night—some he remembers having heard his father sing. The words are all old, and the meanings of some of them have been forgotten.

"Each time I say a prayer for my father's guidance and help," Andrew says, "and usually everything goes OK. I think he is over there in the spirit world. The spirits are just out there. I can go anywhere, take cornmeal and say prayers—by the ocean, to the great waters—it doesn't matter. I can take a little food in a restaurant, say a prayer, taking the food for the spirit. I put the food offering down and don't eat it, or at home we can put it anywhere, even outside. All this time you are making prayers for yourself, no one will know."

"I have made pottery a long time on the mesa. It comes out exactly the same as Lucy's—same shape, same color—but I use crushed lava." I express surprise that men make pottery. Andrew replies that he still farms, and he is building a house on the mesa, but he's more interested in potting. "In the last few years it's been all right for men to do. I started out making clay buffalos, after looking at the one on the nickel. Now I'm learning big pots. Lucy says it is fine for me to be making pots."

Andrew asked his mother how to make big pots. She told him to work only from the outside, never the inside, to keep the form, and to be certain that the piece was straight and level at all times. Andrew has been up since four o'clock this morning, working by kerosene lamp on a large pot—the biggest he has ever tried. We have measured it, and it is fifteen inches high and seventeen wide. For several days, he has been thinking about the decoration, looking at photographs of historic Acoma pots in journals, imagining how certain motifs will fit on this form and working out the colors—orange, black, and brown—for the decoration to go on the white background.

Now, as we return from the store, he looks forward to working on it again by lamplight. The glow of the gas lantern is almost the color of the alpenglow that we have seen the last few evenings at sunset: an iridescent pink the depth of a pearl, shimmering in the stillness, and turning for a few moments to bright gold on the mesas. It has moved us, and we have mentioned it often. Andrew sits down to his pot.

"I want people to know I make pottery, that I make it with no help. Some men, they help their wives in some ways, but actually it is the women who make most of the pottery. I went to art school in Denver and I have a little training in drawing and commercial art. I really enjoy painting on my pottery—finding the old designs, adapting them to my round shapes, or figuring out how certain ones will fit certain pots. I enjoyed painting these designs for your book so much that I may take up painting, too!"

Andrew signs his work "Drew Lewis," with a half-circle over it, like an arc of sunshine.

W RITING A SIMPLE, CONCISE SYNOPSIS of Lucy's and the Pueblo people's pottery heritage has proved much more difficult than I at first thought possible. It seemed reasonable to me that a survey and paraphrase of books on this subject would allow a succinct picture of Pueblo pottery history to emerge. What confronted me instead was an ocean of detail, some cautious generalizations, and conflicting opinions about such major events as the first manufacture of pottery by the ancestors of the Pueblo. Still, some idea of Lucy's artistic heritage is of value here, and, willy-nilly, I attempt to give one.

Pueblo pottery has been exhaustively classified and analyzed. The result is a proliferation of pottery types that may have great value for the specialist, but which to the nonspecialist is a dazzling exercise in uselessness. Yet, such an imposing display of terms and types and classifications could hardly be squeezed out of a limited or impoverished pottery industry. In the American Southwest is one of mankind's richest, most artistically fertile pottery traditions.

Opinion seems to be that pottery did not originate independently in the Southwest, but that the basic technology was imported from Mexico. The first pottery in the Southwest is thought to date from about 300 B.C. In the ancestral Pueblo region (the upper San Juan River basin), one school claims a date round about the time of

Christ, and another gives about A.D. 500 for the first pottery production. These early pots were undecorated and are called "brownwares" by archaeologists.

There were three "cultures" in the Southwest in the two millennia between 500 B.C. and A.D. 1500, of which only one—the Anasazi—is thought to be directly ancestral to the modern Pueblo people. In south and central Arizona, the culture identified as the Hohokam existed from about 300 B.C. to A.D. 1400. This group displayed many Mesoamerican traits, including complex and sophisticated irrigation, manufacture of pottery and jewelry, and copper casting. They also had some trade contact with the south, and acted as the first filter in North America through which Mesoamerican ideas were modified before reaching the other two cultures existing in the Southwest. In the early fifteenth century, for unknown reasons, the Hohokam ceased to exist as a cultural entity.

The region of eastern Arizona and west-central New Mexico was occupied by a culture called the Mogollan from about 200 B.C. to A.D. 1200. They made pottery different from neighboring peoples, and the archaeological record indicates a complex social development, which books describe as "little understood." Though the Mogollan, along with the Hohokam, acted as agents or filters for disseminating some Mesoamerican techniques and traits to their northern neighbors, the Anasazi, after about A.D. 900 the direction of influence was reversed. The final phase of Mogollan culture is known as Mimbres (1050–1200) and is characterized by apartmentlike dwellings of up to three stories with many rooms and a highly sophisticated black-on-white pottery. In the thirteenth century, the Mogollan villages were all abandoned for unknown reasons. It is thought that the Mogollan may have become entirely acculturated and simply blended into the Anasazi population.

The Anasazi, considered the ancestors of the Pueblo people, lived in the Four Corners region—where the corners of Utah, Colorado, Arizona, and New Mexico meet. Archaeological evidence shows that they appeared in this area about the time of Christ, with already highly developed basketry techniques and a hunting and gathering economy with incipient agriculture. There are seven conventional Anasazi periods—Basketmaker I–III and Pueblo I–IV—which are described differently by different authorities. These periods or phases are based on general criteria of cultural change and do not have a one-to-one correspondence with ceramic types or aesthetic considerations. The historic period begins about 1600, after the Spanish presence began to be felt.

Whether the Anasazi were indigenous inhabitants whose way of living changed or were immigrants into the Four Corners area is not known. A compromise theory is that the early Anasazi people were both natives and newcomers. A plain brown pottery is one of the traits that defines the Anasazi. These brownwares resemble earlier Mogollan brownwares, and whether or not the early Anasazi potters were in fact Mogollan immigrants has not been determined. This early pottery was made using essentially the same techniques employed by the Pueblo potters today. Graywares developed from brownwares, though brownware production continued locally long after graywares had spread to become the predominant Anasazi pottery type and even after decorated pots had appeared. Brown- and graywares were undecorated, but polished surfaces appear around A.D. 400, and pot shapes show great refinement, even though they remain basically simple. In some areas, undecorated, plain wares continued to be made up to modern times.

The earliest known instances of corrugated pots are not cited in my sources, but apparently this type of pot became more popular than smooth-surfaced wares in the period between A.D. 850 and 1000. Corrugation—that is, allowing the coils on the pot surface to remain unsmoothed—allows a wide range of decorative possibilities. Decorative effects produced by using different techniques of corrugation and by combining smooth and corrugated areas were fabricated in large numbers.

Painted decoration on pottery appears about A.D. 600 among the Anasazi, manifesting as a black pigment on a gray or white clay. (The use of white slip appears in the middle eighth century.) This basic decorative technique—black paint on a white ground—was explored, extrapolated, and exploited with a vigor that is awesome. Among these black-on-white pots are some of the greatest expressions in pottery that man has produced.

The period between 850 and 1250 saw the development of communities housed in multistoried and -roomed structures—the pueblos. These existed alongside scattered villages of individual pit houses and also isolated homesteads. Though ceramic production was widespead, it is not known whether it was a general household activity or whether it was limited to certain areas or villages or specialists. This period also saw a growth in population, the greatest development of black-on-white pottery, and the ceramic, architectural, and social achievements of the large communities of Mesa Verde and Chaco Canyon.

While the black-on-white tradition developed and maintained its integrity, black decoration on red- or orange-firing clays appeared in the eighth century. From this it is a small step to add another color and make polychrome ware. Black and red ochre pigments and white slip were used on red- and orange- and eventually yellow-firing clays. Some polychrome seems to have appeared in the eighth century, but the tradition did not become widespread until the twelfth and thirteenth centuries. Most of the early polychromes show either simple outlining of a design by another color or one color used for decoration of a pot's interior and a different color for the exterior.

A technique that appeared sporadically in prehistoric pots but took on more importance later is the use of true glaze decoration. Lead minerals with a low fluxing temperature were used locally to decorate pots, but were never utilized to cover an entire pot surface to make it impervious. This use of glaze becomes more common in historic period polychrome of the Rio Grande valley.

In the fourteenth century, the Anasazi underwent large-scale population shifts and changes, which are reflected in the pottery of the time. This is when Mesa Verde was abandoned and the Chaco Canyon area population dwindled. The subsequent two centuries saw the regrouping of the population and the association of peoples with specific areas, as compared to the more diffuse spread of population that had obtained earlier. At this time also, Acoma developed ties with both the Zuni and Zia communities, ties that could not help but influence Acoma pottery. The fourteenth century also saw the beginning of the great florescence of polychrome pottery.

Though the appearance of the Spanish was of momentous import and ushered in the historic period, artistically this event was not as important as the profound upheaval caused by the Pueblo Rebellion of 1680 and the reconquest of the area by the Spanish in 1692. The effects of the Rebellion and reconquest created a disruption of settlements and movement of people, resulting in the communities known today. In general, after this time, potting traditions became more local and were identified with specific communities. After 1820, pots made at a given pueblo can be identified. Glaze decoration disappeared entirely within a half-century of the reconquest.

Acoma pueblo was already an ancient settlement when the Spanish arrived. This fact implies that the Acoma artistic tradition has a similar continuity. The influence of the Spanish cannot but have been profound, whether in the introduction of European design motifs or in religious and political supression. The Acoma pots made from 1600 to 1900 are mainly functional forms lavishly embellished with busy, lyrical poly-chrome designs. Lucy makes most of the utilitarian shapes that were important during the historic period. These are:

Storage jars for grain or water. These large, heavy jars remained in back rooms or in kivas; numerous examples of these vessels exist in museums today because they received the best of care in pueblo life.

Bowls for bread dough, for washing hair, for baby bathing, for kiva food, for prayer cornmeal are rare today because they were easily broken in use.

Water jars for scooping water from cisterns or for carrying on the head.

Canteens for taking water to the fields or for carrying on horseback. These narrow-necked, flat-bodied jugs with two handles to hold a carrying cord were stoppered with corncobs. This form also has ceremonial function.

Pitchers have a single handle but no pouring lip; used for drinking or pouring.

Seed jars are spherical pots with a small mouth and are for storing seeds.

Much Pueblo pottery was and is associated with closely guarded rituals and beliefs. Pottery was considered sacred. Conservative in spirit, potters adhered to their ancestral traditions of decoration. Lucy and other innovative potters of this century are not unique in utilizing inspiration from the far past. This same phenomenon occurred many times in Pueblo pottery history. The term "regressive" often used to describe this phenomenon has unfortunate negative overtones, since it is used to mean the opposite of "progressive." In fact, Lucy, and, one can conjecture, perhaps many of her antecedent potters who drew upon past ceramic achievement, fertilized and brought new vigor to their craft and society. The decorative motifs—animals, birds, feathers, floral designs, clouds, sun, and the like—and geometric patterns touch the heart of the Pueblo world. They are given continuity and importance when enlivened by the genius of a true artist who revitalizes the pottery tradition.

Toward the end of the nineteenth century, individual forays into aesthetic expression began to emerge. Old Nampeyo of Hopi decorated pots with yellow and red feather designs, an innovation at the time, but in fact a revival of a prehistoric style. Later, Maria Martinez of San Ildefonso pueblo begn a blackware tradition that has many followers among contemporary potters. It began from a group of ancient shards excavated on the Pajarito plateau near her home. Lucy Lewis, a few decades younger than Maria, worked from the start in the manner of her ancestors.

37. Acoma pueblo officials in 1936, holding canes of office. Toribio Lewis, first fiscale, is third from the right, next to Father Lambert; others are Roy Chavez, second from right; Estavan Cerno, third from left; Batista Ray, second from left; James T. Vallo, governor, far left. 38. Toribio Lewis, his mother and his sister Lola and brother-in-Law James T. Vallo. 39. The young Lucy, after her marriage.

40. "Beloved Dad, August 19, 1946, Gallup Ceremonial," is the inscription on this photograph from the scrapbook of one of Lucy's daughters.   41. Toribio mounting his horse, Acoma mesa, 1930.   42. Lucy's stepfather, the late Marie Chino's brother John Zieu.

43. Toribio as Second Field Chief, 1950. 44. Lucy and Toribio with their grandson Leland Mitchell, 1955. 45. Lucy's mother and stepfather, her stepsister Mae, and three stepnieces.

46. Lucy with one daughter and two nieces in San Francisco, 1947.　**47.** Lucy and daughter Belle.

48. Lucy making pots in the house on the mesa, 1980.   49. Lucy paints a miniature jar with fine-line pattern, ca. 1960.   50. Lucy, ca. 1950.

51. Lucy Lewis at the Santa Fe Fiesta, 1960, with a wonderful array of pots for sale, including ones that just won award ribbons.   **52.** Two celebrated potters, Maria Martinez and Lucy Lewis, at the opening of the Seven Families exhibition at the Maxwell Museum, Albuquerque.

54. Lucy with HRH Prince Rainier and Princess Grace and their daughters Caroline and Stephanie, at Jemez pueblo, 1976. Also in the picture are Belle (far left) and Stanley Lucero (behind princess), Emma (behind prince) and Lee Mitchell (behind Andrew), Dolores (on Lucy's right), and Andrew Lewis (far right).   **55.** Lucy and her mother, Lola, at the house on the mesa, 1968.   **56.** Lucy selling pots at Old Town, Albuquerque, early 1960s.   **57.** Lucy holding a black-on-white pot.   **58.** Lucy in Washington, D.C., 1979, after her workshop at Wolftrap, Virginia.

59. Lucy (1982) shows how she used to carry water from the cisterns to the house on the mesa.   60. Lucy and daughters selling pots at a benefit for a monastery at Valyermo, California, 1974.   61. Lucy, with Emma, Dolores, and Andrew, making a presentation of one of her pots to Dr. Arthur Turner, a founder of Northwood Institute, Midland, Michigan, for their museum, 1983.   62. Lucy receiving the Woman of Achievement Award from Northwood Institute at ceremonies in Houston, Texas, 1983.

63. Lucy in front of her house at Sky City. 64. She readies an offering of fruit for the saint on the feast day. 65. Making pots in the kitchen at Sky City. 66. Lucy has worn her hair this way since she was young.

67, 68. Lucy in her corn and melon field and near where the pots
are fired. 69. Teaching at the Idyllwild School of Music and the
Arts, California. 70. Shards found on the Acoma Reservation. 71.
Lucy contemplating a finished pot with intense concentration.

72–74. Lucy with her own and old Acoma pots, browsing through the collection at the School of American Research, Indian Arts Research Center, Santa Fe.

75. At Indian Market, Santa Fe, 1983. 76. Forming a water jar; daughter Emma's hand touches the lip. 77. Lucy loves bright-colored shawls. 78. Most pots begin with a finger-pinched form. 79. Lucy sits with queenly grace at the opening of a gallery exhibition featuring her work.

80. Lucy presents one of her pots to Dr. Arthur Turner for the Museum at Northwood Institute, Midland, Michigan, prior to receiving the Woman of Achievement award in Houston, Texas, November 1983. Daughter Dolores watches.   81. Ivan Lewis makes the acceptance speech as Lucy receives the Governor's Award from New Mexico's governor, Toney Anaya, in the capitol rotunda, Santa Fe, October 1983.   82. Lucy holds the plaque presented to her by Governor Anaya.

83. Lee Mitchell, Emma's husband, with grandchild on cradleboard. 84. Ceremonial bows and arrows with photograph of Lucy and award at White House. 85. Kachinas and ceremonial pots. 86. Merle Garcia and his mother, Dolores; Ivan Lin; Valerie Mitchell, her mother, Emma, and brother Seth at opening of Lucy's Houston gallery exhibition. 88, 89. Great-grandchildren. 87, 90. Acoma elementary school parade, Lucy's great-grandchildren participating.

91. Emma's house. Pots given to family members on ceremonial occasions. 92. One of her grandchildren watches Emma make pottery. 93. A hot air balloon over Acoma pueblo on a feast day. 94–96. Corn drying, and grinding dried corn. Chili peppers from the garden.

97–101. Lucy and Emma form 162 loaves of ceremonial bread. The oven is fired, the ash removed, the the loaves are quickly put into the hot oven with a long-handled paddle. After baking about an hour, the bread is removed.

102. Lucy and two of her children selling pots by the side of old Highway 66, ca. 1930. 103. Deer Dance at Mount Taylor elementary school, 1970, with Emma's children dancing. 104. Lucy, daughter Dolores in chili wagon, her sister-in-law Lupe, and her cousen Eva (Helice Vallo's daughter) with daughter Hilda, ca. 1940. 105. Acoma Officers' Feast, 1950, taken by one of the children at Lucy's house on the mesa.

106–110. Ivan Lewis, Lucy's firstborn, and his wife, Rita, live at Cochiti pueblo and make traditional pottery figures. 111–13. Each figure is fired individually. It is placed on a raised grill and covered with a wire dome, over which cow chips are arranged. Wood beneath the grill is ignited and burns about a half hour. It takes all day to fire a group of figures. 114. One of Rita's "storyteller" figures.

115. Andrew Lewis. 116. Emma Lewis Mitchell. 117. Dolores Lewis Garcia. 118. Dolores, Emma, Lucy, and Andrew at the exhibition opening in Houston, each with his or her pot. 119. Stanley and Belle Lewis Lucero and daughter.

120. Ivan Lewis in his Santa Fe Indian School track team sweater.   121. Andrew Lewis perches on the ladder of one of the houses on the mesa.   122. Dolores Lewis Garcia with one of Lucy's pots.   123. Emma Lewis Mitchell in ceremonial dress, with pottery she has made.

124. Tularosa Black-on-white pitcher, ca. 1100–1300.   **125.** Escavada Black-on-white jar, ca. 950–1100.

126. Socorro, Rio Grande Valley, A.D. 1100–1200. H. 38.1 cm. 127. Ako polychrome, ca. 1700. H. 29.2 cm. 128. Ako polychrome, ca. 1730. H. 27 cm. 129. Acoma, ca. 1910. H. 27.9 cm.

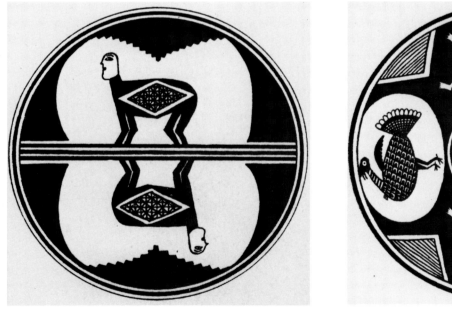

130–33. Designs from Mimbres pottery, ca. 900.

134, 135. Designs from Mimbres pottery, ca. 900.   **136.** Mimbres Black-on-white bowl, ca. 1000–1100.

137. Jar, parrot design, 1910. H. 28.3 cm.

138. Jar with lugs, spike pattern, 1900. H. 25.4 cm.   139. Polychrome jar with lugs, 1900. H. 24.7 cm.   140. Bowl, 1925. D. 12.8 cm.   141. Polychrome jar, floral pattern, 1910. H. 28.3 cm.

142. Escavada Black-on-white bird effigy pitcher, ca. 950–1100.   143. Gallup Black-on-white bowl, ca. 950–1100.   144, 145. Mesa Verde Black-on-white mugs, ca. 1000. Both H. 13.7 cm.

146. Mimbres Red-on-white bowl, antelope design, ca. 900–1000. D. 27.5 cm.   147. Mimbres Black-on-white bowl, ca. 1000–1150.   148. Mimbres Black-on-white bowl, man and woman under a blanket design, ca. 900–1000. D. 26.3 cm.   149. Mimbres Black-on-white bowl, bird design, ca. 900–1000. D. 28.7 cm.

150–52. Polychrome jar, Acoma, 1910–20. H. 34.3 cm.   153. Historic Acoma, ca. 1750. H. 25 cm.   154. Acoma, ca. 1950. H. 27.3 cm.

155. Socorro Black-on-white jar, ca. 1075–1250.

MAKING POTTERY

ACOMA CLAY IS A MYSTERY. FROM my first contacts with the Lewis family I have known that they were unlikely ever to let me see where they dig the clay. Lucy and the girls talk constantly of the clay, as they work with it: how hard it is to get, how sometimes it is more coarse, what the impurities are, how hard it is to refine, the bits of calcium that can pop out of a piece long after firing.

"For the clay you have to walk about eight miles back, west of the pueblo mesa. No one has ever been there but Acomas. We couldn't take anyone else there, we just couldn't," Dolores says. "I am scared to go myself; I suppose I haven't been there for twenty years. Everyone gathers his or her own clay, but sometimes—like with me— the lady sends some man in the family; sometimes the potter's children go to the sacred place, the dangerous pit in the ground. Of course the clay is heavy, and it has to be hauled a long way. We could build a road, but we think someone would come and take the clay, so we don't."

Lucy and Toribio used to get the clay together. It was an arduous climb, even then, and some years ago the mine partly collapsed. It is more risky now, Lucy observes, "You never know when a rock will fall."

121

The clay comes out of the mine in slabs that they say look like hard-packed mud, but which fall apart into chunks after being brought up to the open air. Lucy has an old hand-cranked grinding machine. I have watched some of the men use it with perhaps twenty pounds of clay at a time, laboriously breaking down the difficult material. The small chunks are then ground to a powder on a metate.

"There's a prayer that goes into digging the clay, there's a prayer that goes into refining it. There's a prayer for making the pots, and maybe two prayers for bringing them to the dealer," says Emma with a smile.

The powdered clay is soaked in water. Impurities come to the surface and are poured off, several times. In the old days the clay was dried on the rooftops of the adobe houses on the mesa; now the women lay it on cookie sheets in the sun. The dried slurry is ground again on a metate, then screened several times through nylon mesh window curtains or fine wire mesh.

It takes a whole day for each step in the preparation of the clay, if there are no interruptions. Usually, because there are interruptions, two or three days are required for each step. The women process only enough clay to make a few pots at a time, so the refining must be repeated frequently. Often I have heard them say that no pots could be made because the clay was not ready. Clay mixing is a process that is always in progress at some stage.

Everyone prospects for pottery shards on the mesa and in the fields. These are soaked overnight and pounded on a hard stone, then ground on a flat metate and screened to a fine power. This is used as temper in the clay body, to reduce thermal shock in the firing. Another day is spent preparing the shards. Emma explains that it is a struggle to find the scarce old pot fragments, and the Lewises recycle shards from pots that blow up in the firing. Andrew says, "It's nice to think of your ancestors' pots in your pots."

After the second grinding, the clay powder with ground shard temper is mixed to plastic consistency. There are different methods. Emma mounds it out on the floor several inches high, makes a hole in the center, pours water in, and kneads it over and over, on her hands and knees, until she is satisfied with the feel of it. Andrew and Dolores mix their batches with water in dishpans, kneading the clay and transferring it to the floor for wedging with their bare feet. This is the way Lucy always did it. Dolores now prepares the clay her mother uses.

Dolores remembers that it took a long time to learn everything, and they learned over and over by trial and error. "Like the first times Emma and I tried to grind clay. Our hands hurt. I felt like I was wearing metal gloves. Lucy could tell us, but she wanted us to learn by ourselves."

When the clay body is mixed, it should sit for a week before it is used. The pulverized shards expand in the moisture, and a homogeneous mixture is made. The potters know the difference in plasticity between freshly mixed clay and clay that has been allowed to mature.

The wet clay is dark gray, but it fires white. Its geological formation is a mystery to me; my potter's instinct says that it is an impure kaolin—it handles like one—but it is too coarse. It must contain a good deal of alkali because it seems quite hard after firing and rings like crystal. It may be part talc, similar to the clay-talc body used by the ancient Egyptians. The idea of a chemical analysis is repugnant to the Indians; they would rather believe that the clay is a special mixture put there uniquely for their use, which, in fact, is true.

The white clay used for the polishing coat is very rare, found in only one place that the Acomas know. It is even harder to fetch than the body clay. The Lewises tell of a long trek over the hills, up to a mountain where there is a secret cave with an opening so small that only someone small can enter. Inside, the hard clay must be pickaxed off the rock walls. Emma shows me a plastic sack about six inches around that took all day to mine, declaring that this clay is so precious she hides it in her bedroom where no one can find it.

This must be kaolin. It is a whitish color in the raw state, but varies in purity. "We can tell when a batch of the clay is purer," the potters say, "when it will be better. Sometimes it is not as fine, or not as pure looking, and sure enough, it won't stick on the pot. It falls off before firing or it flakes off afterwards, or it isn't the right white." The clay for polishing comes in chunks, which are pulverized and slaked in water to painting consistency. If impurities come to the surface of the water, the clay is washed again.

"We believe in the power of the clay," stresses Dolores. "We ask our own people to taste the clay and to taste the white slip. When we give demonstrations we also ask the students to do that. It smells so good, it tastes so fresh. We make a prayer when we take the clay and when we use it. The pots are spirits. The clay is sacred. You can eat it raw, and you are going back to it when you die."

"Our children come by the table when we are working or painting and put their fingers into the clay or the pigment to taste, one at a time, the white slip, the ochre, the brown paint, the clay body. Even our house cats climb up to drink the white slip." Emma adds, "Last week I forgot to cover the paint stone in my kitchen. I guess one of the kittens was hungry because I could see tracks on the oilcloth where it had been drinking the paint."

A white enamel washpan piled full of prepared clay will last Dolores all summer. Her mother will use much more. The problems of procuring and mixing that clay are astonishing. The quality of the clay varies; sometimes it cannot be used. Refining procedures may fail. In forming pots, great care must be taken to keep the pieces from breaking. "Now you know why most of the Acoma ladies don't want to do all that," Emma says. "It's just too hard, so they use commercial stuff."

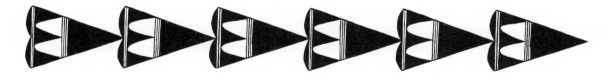

MAKING POTS

Lucy is one of the most facile potters I have ever watched; her skills belie her age. With the camera I have been documenting her pot-making for four years, at the pace I think Indians normally do claywork, which is irregular at best. In the fall of 1983, Lucy needed to prepare for two major exhibitions—a new and unusual requirement in her life. During this time I came to the pueblo at ten-day intervals and stayed for five days at a time. Lucy worked steadily for three months, completing a group of pieces the girls agreed were the best they had ever seen. She used each style of the past forty years of potting; this period represents her "contemporary" work, as opposed to the "earlier" work done during the three decades before that.

Lucy did not make any of the large storage vessels and water jars for which historic Acoma is known; that would have been her mother's and her aunt Helice's province. Her own generation bridged the making of strictly ceremonial pots and utilitarian containers and the making of wares for sale. That she was able to earn the appreciation of sophisticated buyers and museums is a tribute to her inventiveness, skill, and artistry.

When she finished the pots that autumn, she had made large vessels with traditional orange parrot designs, black fine-line patterned water jars, lidded pots, deer decorations on large and small bowls, a wedding vase, canteens, tall forms with variations of the dynamic zigzag motif, crinkle-edge platters, seed pots, and shapes with a "corrugated" texture. Several were in process at once, left around the room so Lucy could look at and think about them as she worked. When one was finished, it was fired and put away in a cupboard, but was often taken out to be looked at again.

Lucy's recognition has come for several reasons: her pots are the best being made today in this particular polychrome tradition; they are of superb artistic quality; and they display a quality best called simply "spirit." She makes pottery within the vigorous potting tradition of her people, yet her pots, fundamentally and essentially, partake of her own vitality and individual energy.

The kitchen table in Dolores' house is Lucy's studio, although she enjoys making pottery by the big wood stove in the house on the mesa. Her tools are simple, and she has had them for years: a few gourd tools—free-form shapes whose edges have been sharpened with a file; an old sharp-edged metal can lid; some smooth pebbles; a short knife; a leather tooling awl; a soft rag; a wooden stick. She keeps them all in a coffee can or a plastic bowl. She works with a great economy of movement, slowly and deliberately turning the clay, adding, subtracting, pinching, and pushing with the experience of seventy years.

Tiny pots, several inches high, begin with a ball of clay finger-pinched into the approximate final shape. Lucy may do twenty or more such pieces at a time—probably not for sale but for ceremonial giving. The rough forms are set aside to stiffen. Later a tiny gourd tool is used to press a curve from the inside out, then another gourd rib will make the reverse curve of the neck, as Lucy pushes inward from the outside.

When the pots are stiff enough, they are scraped roughly with a sharp-edged tin lid then smoothed with the same tool used in criss-cross motions. As dry fissures open up, tiny balls of clay are worked into the cracks with great patience. Each small pot is honed down to a graceful narrow foot, and the bottom is indented, in the manner of vessels to be carried on the head. Lucy sets the pots down, one at a time, on the oilcloth directly in front of her and examines them closely. With a sharp, short knife blade she cuts a sliver of clay from the lip as she turns the piece gently with her fingers, evening and leveling the lip.

Lucy works in groups of pots—two, four, or eight—but never so many that she tires of the shapes. She alternates larger vessels with smaller ones in the forming period, and generally at least two are similar in form. She paces herself, sitting quietly, working steadily for perhaps an hour. Suddenly she stops, puts her hands in her lap, gazes at the piece in front of her and those she has already done. Then she pushes herself up away from the table and moves to warm her hands by the fireplace or walks in slow circles around the room.

Lucy has a number of fired saucers of varying diameters and heights; some are the broken bottoms of old jars and some she has made. These hollow forms support new wet pots. In Tewa, the language of some eastern pueblos, this support is called a *puki*; in Keresan, it is a *huditzi*. A special pecan wood salad bowl from the Ozarks, some wheel-thrown bowls made by Anglo potters, and even round plastic containers sometimes serve the same purpose, and she has a number of these stacked on the floor. Most pots larger than palm size require a *huditzi*.

SEED POTS

Seed pots seem to hold a special place among the pots that Lucy makes. She revived the form from ancient ceremonial pots. This shape is meant to hold a few seeds from a particular crop, which either will be planted the next season or are simply symbolic. The volume of this spherical container seems to be expanding, like a small balloon. The mouth is nearly closed, being large enough for one corn kernel to slip through but not for a mouse to enter.

I never saw Lucy make this shape except in the old house at Sky City, although I do not know if that is significant. She begins a seed pot by fisting a rather large ball of clay into a semiglobular form in one palm, then lets this stiffen. On a pine board on her lap, she rolls a fat coil several feet long, pinching it and slapping it in her palms to start, then rolling with her fingers arched up and the flat of one palm moving quickly back and forth. As the coil lengthens, she uses both palms, moving from the center out to the ends.

The first clay shape, now stiffer, goes into the *huditzi* Lucy has chosen from among the ones at hand. She fits the pot to the supporting form, lifts a coil, touches one end to the lip of the rough shape, and pinches the joint with thumb and forefinger. She rotates the *huditzi* as she lays the long coil down little by little, holding the tail up in her left hand. Pushing down with her fingers, she joins the seam. The rotation is reversed, and her fingers seal the joint again as she goes the opposite way.

Holding her left hand inside, she smooths and shapes with sweeping motions, turning the pot. She uses a gourd tool to work inside. Scraping in both directions

125

stretches the clay and thins it. She adds the next coil, set inward from the last one, and joins it to the first by rotating the pot twice, once in each direction. The pot is bulged and refined with rapid movements of the moistened gourd tool. More coils and more pressure make the shape bloom. Lucy often checks the top edge for evenness and cuts it straight with the knife.

She leans back on the sofa, arms folded against her blue sweater, and looks down at the pot on the board, squinting to get the line of the form. She holds this pose about ten minutes, silently concentrating all her mental energies on the pot. The clay is stiff enough to receive the next coil. She rolls it, applies it, and joins it to the pot.

Suddenly she picks the pot up out of the *huditzi* with both hands, and takes it in her lap. The fingers of her left hand inside, she pats the shoulder curve in with her right hand, at almost a 45 degree angle. Then she returns it to the *huditzi,* deftly drawing the shoulder up and in and thinning the clay wall. Now she plops it upside down in her lap and, with the gourd tool, pulls the base to a narrow foot, improving the grace and lilt of the form. No matter how much she slaps the wet clay around, it returns to symmetry when she cuddles and pats it right side up. This never ceases to astonish me.

With upward movements of the gourd tool she nearly closes the top of the pot. Her thumb and fingertips pinch the edge round and even. Finished, she leaves the piece directly in front of her while she looks at it, turns it slowly, and gives it a few taps. Then she pushes it aside on the board, out of her line of vision, leans back against the sofa, arms crossed, and goes to sleep.

When the pot is leather-hard, it is scraped and smoothed with water. Lucy waits until she has a group of pots and scrapes them all, cradling each piece in her lap or against her breast and sweeping the sharp can lid in diagonal motions back to front. The pot is rotated briefly and scraped quickly. When this refinement is accomplished, she changes the rotation and begins scraping again, thus compressing and strengthening the clay wall as well as perfecting the curve.

Scraped pots are set aside to get a bit drier and tougher. To water-smooth the surface, Lucy moistens a rock and rubs it vigorously over the clay, adding water with her fingers to make it more slippery. Water-smoothing works best with horizontal movements around the pot, working from the top down. The stone is moistened many times. It may take several hours for the quick back-and-forth movements to create a totally smooth surface. Making ten pots of average size, scraping, and smoothing can easily take two or three weeks.

CORRUGATED POTS

Many of the shards Lucy picked up as a young girl on the mesa were in the exposed-coil and corrugated texture style found among the ancient vessels. Traditionally, the corrugated pots were cooking pots. At one time, the Pueblo people coated them with pitch when they were still hot from the fire, to make them waterproof. Some of Lucy's corrugated pieces are fired so that decorative smoky clouds appear at some places on the light-colored pots. This is one of the most arduous of Lucy's styles. It is almost essential to have someone else roll the coils while she does the building.

Dolores has made clay especially for the piece Lucy is starting today, with more water than usual, to make it soft enough for pressing. The bottom part of the corrugated pot takes so long, Lucy says, that when it is finally fixed in the *huditzi* the rest takes shape in comparatively no time at all. She looks on quietly as Dolores rolls the first coil, long and thin, across the table.

Lucy picks up one end and begins to wind it into a flat spiral against the table, squeezing gently so clay sticks to clay. This part is important, or the pot will leak. To keep the pattern, the coils must remain round, symmetrical, and even. When the corrugated pancake is seven or eight inches wide, she cradles it in her palm, testing it for strength. Laying it on the table again, she uses the sharp cedar tool, with its tiny incised pattern, to make a textured pattern on each coil perpendicular to the seam line.

She chooses a *huditzi* and puts the coiled pancake in it. Dolores, rolling another long skinny coil, sighs: "Last year about this time we were up in the mountains piñon picking." I know she is eager to break the silence, and we talk about the wonderful taste of piñon nuts, the difficulty of gathering and shucking them, and the unusual flavor they have when they are roasted. This is really the piñon season: Dolores rises and brings back a small basket from which each of us takes a few nuts.

Lucy picks up the new coil, swirling it, squeezing it gently so it will adhere to the one before. Dolores is rolling faster now, to keep up. Emma joins, and the pace quickens. She holds the coil up while Lucy does the attaching, and the pot rapidly widens. Lucy smooths the interior coils with the gourd tool, careful to avoid blemishing the exterior texture. In order to texture newly added coils, Lucy shoves the bowl so that part of its surface extends above the *huditzi,* allowing her to use the wooden tool on the clay. Dolores is rolling coils as fast as Emma and Lucy can handle them, all the same length and thickness.

The newly formed bowl shape is transferred to a taller *huditzi* for extra support. The piece is becoming more vertical, and Lucy can texture it now without needing to change its position. Dolores laughs, breaking the concentration in the room. She is reminded of the old tomcat that one day climbed unnoticed into a big corrugated pot of Lucy's drying on the floor. Later they spotted movement inside the pot, and thinking it was a snake, they were almost ready to break the pot to rid the house of it when the cat climbed out. The cat often plays with the miniature animals the women make, rolling them around on the floor.

Lucy decides to rest; she has been working for three hours without stopping. In Keresan she tells Dolores to texture the coils she has just added. She would not allow her daughter to build the form itself, but she will let her texture it with the pointed cedar tool. I watch as Dolores makes the marks: they are not the same as Lucy's, and now the piece takes on a random spontaneity. Lucy leaves to rest, and the group disperses. Dolores picks up one of the small pots on the floor, to scrape and water-smooth it.

Emma it known for her small platters, decorated with Mimbres-style animals. Pounding a flat clay pancake in her palm, she widens and deepens it with the gourd tool, from the center out to the edge. She puts it aside and begins another, until there are eight. Turning each one between her fingers, she refines the circle and the thickness. She taps the plates against the table to flatten the base. The clay will stiffen soon, for scraping and smoothing, or she will take them home to finish. They will be decorated at some later time with rabbits, turtles, deer, flute-player figures, and combinations of these, in black lines on the white ground.

Emma's own kitchen in her house below the mesa, where she usually makes her pots, is a thoroughfare for children playing, getting drinks, investigating the refrigerator, washing their hands in the sink, and looking for things to do. When Lucy is there, some of them pull at grandmother's sleeve; others fend for themselves. From time to time Emma looks up from her potting, admonishes one, praises another for handling a situation, answering a constant flow of questions. Somehow the delicate, exacting work she does with fingers or brush meshes happily with the bustle around her.

Dolores is known for small canteens, which are put together from two deep platter forms similar to Emma's plates. While we wait for Lucy, she fashions sixteen such rounds, which will form eight vessels when they are joined. A neck and two small handles will be added to each. She decorates the finished work with her own versions of the Mimbres animals or with geometric designs, in black and white with orange accents. Dolores does not keep up with the demand for her canteens because, as she says, she has too much else to do.

Lucy returns to finish the corrugated pot. Dolores rolls, Emma holds, and Lucy attaches the remaining coils, until the jar is ten inches high. She puts her hand down inside, pushing out gently to bulge the curve of the jar, enlarging the volume and merging the line of the belly with the neck. Then she adds the finishing texture marks with the wooden tool. Sitting back in the chair, she fixes her gaze on the whole form, drinking it in for an interminable time while no one speaks a word. Occasionally she turns it. Finally she gets up and says it is finished.

Coiling a Big Pot

Other potters today at Acoma make jars twice as big as Lucy's. Size is not a major consideration for her. The largest wares she ever made, according to her daughters, she made this autumn for the gallery exhibition in Houston. Lucy claims that when she was young she was advised by an old lady who made big pots never to make large pieces. The old lady, arthritic and hunched over, said, "Don't make these, you'll look like me, and big pots may blow up in firing." Lucy states that she took that lady's word for years.

I watched two large water jars being polished and decorated—one with the parrot design, one of fine-line decoration, each about fourteen inches high and equally wide—but I did not see them made. I ask Lucy if she can build a big pot while I am there, for photographic documentation; she nods, smiles, and says that she will try a bigger one next time. We agree on a date, because she needs to set aside three or four days for the endeavor, and Dolores has to be free to prepare the clay.

We begin on the appointed day at 7:00 A.M., in Dolores' house. On the kitchen table are five or six *huditzi*s of different size. Lucy moves them about, cogitating. A large pile of clay is under plastic wraps on the floor. No one has had breakfast, or even coffee, but Lucy is ready to work. She breaks off a chunk of clay, pounding it with her fist to form a soft floppy bowl, then drops it into one of the support shapes. It fills the *huditzi,* so she quickly moves it to a larger one. Emma and Dolores roll fat coils, about two inches high and a quarter of an inch thick, which they flatten on both sides and help Lucy string out, adding one on top of the other to the initial shape.

In this way the bowl quickly grows by three coils; each coil is laid a bit outside the last to widen the curve as it builds. Suddenly the pot is bigger than the *huditzi*; Lucy puts her arms around it and lifts it gingerly into the next larger size. She smooths the coils together with her fingers, then uses a moistened gourd tool, pulling it toward her with fast strokes first, turning the pot. Then she applies the tool with crisscross movements like an "X," back and forth, until the coil lines are obliterated. She smooths both interior and exterior with the tool and trues the symmetry of the diameter and the curve.

Lucy stands up to peer inside, looks at the profile, moves her head around for a general view. Holding the gourd tool in her left hand, she reaches inside and begins to bulge out the form, turning the pot as she goes. The shape is swelling gracefully. Dolores says Lucy really has fun with big pots, but they take so much clay that it is impossible to do many.

Lucy asks for more coils, and the girls quickly roll and flatten the next two. Emma holds up the end of one, resting the weight of it on her shoulder while Lucy lays it in position. Dolores picks up the next, and the process is repeated. The pot stands about eight inches higher than the large *huditzi,* which is as it should be—except the clay is soft and construction has been hurried. We gasp as the pot begins to collapse.

The women mutter to each other in Keresan, scurrying around the piece, bolstering the clay with their hands, but their efforts are ineffective. The pot is simply too big for the support form and too soft to stand alone; it sags above the *huditzi*. I suggest holding it up with a stuffing of wadded newspaper, and they hurry to comply. Dolores scours the kitchen for something else to use for a *huditzi,* but all the pans are too flat bottomed. Lucy utters a loud exclamatory sound and we all turn toward her, amazed at the unusual outburst. She orders Dolores to go up to the mesa immediately and bring back the huge wooden salad bowl she keeps there but has never used. She bought it for a *huditzi*—the Acoma do not generally make big bowls of salad.

Dolores climbs into my rented automobile and we barrel off toward Sky City. If we take too long, the pot will fall apart completely; as we leave, Emma is shoring it up with a dish towel. Reaching the top of the mesa, we dash into Lucy's house, startling Andrew, who is working on a big piece himself at the kitchen table, where books are open to color pictures of old Acoma pots. We rummage through blankets, costumes, bedding, boxes of ceremonial articles, until finally we discover the big pecan wood bowl and jump back in the car for the return trip down.

While we were away, Lucy began working on the water-jar shapes she had fisted and pinched yesterday. Today she puts the four small and two large pieces into *huditzi*s and shapes them out with a tool, bulging from the inside. To reverse the direction for a wide neck, she presses the gourd inward, making a sharp reversal of outline, from a convex to a concave curve, as the piece turns. As we walk in with the bowl, Emma is pinching out clay pancakes for plates. She has recently been experimenting with pots in the shape of nesting birds, in the manner of Mimbres effigies, but that complicated work will need her undivided concentration, so she spends the time waiting for us to return on more familiar forms.

The wooden bowl, eighteen inches wide and seven deep, is lined with a towel. Clay *huditzi*s are porous, and pots do not stick to them; *huditzi*s of other materials require a cloth between the support form and the piece. Four of us lift the big pot from its present *huditzi* to the new one; the corners of the towel are wrapped around the sagging pot and tied on top to support the curve. Lucy decides not to touch it yet; she wants it to stiffen for an hour or so. She glances meaningfully at Dolores, who goes to the kitchen and returns with a stack of cold tortillas and butter, green chili, egg salad, and coffee. We sit at the table among the small pots and the big one, happy to have saved it.

After a time Lucy stands up to gauge the condition of her big challenge. She unties the towel, letting it fall over the sides to the table, lifts out the wads of news-paper, and fingers the wall inside and out. Satisfied, she requests and receives more coils, building the form wider and higher. Then she reaches in with a moistened gourd tool, bellying the clay out against the wood, turning the *huditzi* and moving the tool upwards. The pot stands now about eight or ten inches above the *huditzi*. More turn-ing and smoothing take place. Large cracks developed when the pot was lifted and moved; these must be filled and refined.

When she has made it perfectly round and bowed the curve to the top, the piece looks like a big cone—not yet like an olla. Lucy finds a larger gourd tool, positions it about five inches down from the lip on the outside, and presses it into the clay with her other hand inside. The wooden bowl turns easily on the smooth oilcloth as Lucy makes a symmetrical reverse curve, angling the shape in at the top. The clay has had as much as it can take, she announces; she will wait for tomorrow to cut the lip, enhance the curves, and improve the surface.

The next day the pot is still too moist to work. I went off to see Ivan Lewis at Cochiti, and the ladies rested. On the following morning, the clay is stiff but pliable. Lucy attacks the lip with her knife, cutting a sliver off to even the line. Then she wants it out of the *huditzi*. Her youngest daughter has arrived, and Dolores' sons are here. Four of them take the ends of the towel and lift the pot. Lucy tells them to stop and hold it in the air that way, while she bulges the profile curve again from the inside with a tool. Now she wants it upside down, to scrape.

We look at each other in consternation. Upside down! This big, unwieldy pot? These thin, wet walls? But the ladies regroup, and the piece is turned over with a determined, quick motion. Lucy sighs, and everybody giggles with relief. She begins to work the pot thinner and rounder with her gourd tools. The surface cracks are patched with tiny balls of clay. She scrapes upward, speeding the curve and narrowing the foot, then makes a shallow indentation on the bottom. The rest of the day is spent refining.

Around Lucy eddies a cheerful bustle. A few of the teenagers watch television across the room. Dolores does dishes, puts on more chili, and works intermittently on Lucy's eight-inch water jars, polishing the top edges with a moistened pebble. Jason, a toddler great-grandson, wanders about, crunching crackers and playing precariously with the kitten around the pots on the floor. There are interruptions of food and coffee. Neighbors and neighbors' children come and go. Lucy goes to rest several times but is too excited about her big pot to stay in one place.

Tomorrow the jar will be turned upright again, and the wall will be worked thinner and truer. This is the largest pot Lucy has made. Admitting she is fairly certain of its survival now, she moves one finger over it in the air, in a drawing motion. She is trying out images and directions, mentally shaping her vision of the design. She has done this thousands of times in her potting, and each new form is a new canvas.

POLISHING

Every pot is scraped with a tin can lid, and water-smoothed again and again with water and a pebble. The rapid motions of the stone cause a slurry to form; then it is ready for white slip burnishing. The kaolin has been washed, screened, and allowed to stand in water many days. The water coming to the surface above the silt in the bowl has an oily quality. Lucy lets the kaolin dry in the bowl between uses; fine sand drops to the bottom, and clay particles come to the top. For the best results, only the finest clay particles suspended in water will do.

The white slip is applied with a folded cloth in a thin coating and polished immediately, while it is still wet, with a water-smoothed pebble. After vigorous burnishing, the pot shines, unless the slip is wrong somehow. The white kaolin slip is so thin that gray from the clay body shows through. The process of applying slip is repeated until the built-up coating is opaque and without blemish. Only wet slip can be polished; if the slip is polished further after it dries, it will flake off. Thus, only small areas can be done at a time.

The potters keep favorite stones for polishing. Some pebbles are curved for certain indentations or pointed for corners. The hardest to find is a stone for the big plain curves, where poor polishing technique shows up instantly. Polishing a big pot takes Lucy days because only a little at a time can be done.

Andrew, who has been making vessels just four or five years, admits that he is still a novice at polishing. He chuckles with this story: One day a friend of his who was walking with him in the vicinity of Lucy's mesa house, picked up an old cloth and asked him what it was. "My polishing-slip applicator," replied Andrew. "That's a pretty fancy name," rejoined his friend, "for an old rag."

Painting

Pigments for the designs at Acoma are minerals and metallic compounds in rock form, with the exception of the wild spinach juice—*guaco*—which Emma says will not work alone, nor will the iron-bearing rocks work without it. Lucy and her daughters have told numerous stories about people bringing them rocks, beautiful colored rocks, that they are positive will produce good color—but do not. The ladies do not know what these rocks are, but from long experience they can recognize the correct raw hues and workability of ground pigment. They know when they have a wrong rock. I think that the two rocks they rub together on the metate for black paint contain iron oxide and manganese dioxide, respectively. To this is added the *guaco,* for binding and for color.

Potters understand that nothing in the raw state is the same color it will be when it has been fired. The Acoma know that there is a relationship between the look of the rock and the intensity of hue it develops in the fire. Trained to observe nature and its materials, these potters look for every variable and idiosyncrasy of cause and effect, and then duplicate those they desire. It is an art handed down from one individual to another.

They use a mineral pigment that is ochre-hued before firing and orange afterward, but they call it "yellow paint." Found in arroyos, it is a silt that is already fine but full of sand and must be washed and screened. "There are lots of different yellows," explains Dolores. "If you don't like one, find another. Or mix it. Some are too light, really almost white. You can experiment as much as you want with this. We have tried a great many, but finally we stick to one, and we get it by ourselves. But it all has to be processed. You know, half our time is spent processing things."

"If the yellow paint is too dark to begin with, it will sort of burn or get too dark in the fire," Emma declares. "Some of the yellows will fire almost brick red." That pigment was used a long time ago to cover the cook pots, often with black designs; today the brick red may be used to accent. I believe that what the Indians call yellow paint—the sandy silt—is a form of rutile, impure titanium dioxide. Potters have trouble with its variable oranges even when it is bought in industrial standard form. The Acoma reservation has places with some amounts of uranium and antimony—both burn yellow or orange under certain conditions—which might account for the inconsistencies.

"We get used to one paint grinding stone and we can't use any other," Emma concedes. "We all found our paint stones some special way. When Lucy paints at my house, I share with her, and when I go up to the mesa, she shares with me, but we all have our own ways to grind the rocks. I can't even grind on Dolores' stone because it won't take my way."

The pigment rock is moistened with a little water each time the potter grinds it against the stone to make paint. Emma's grinding technique, I have noticed, is to hold the pigment rock so just one point of it touches the grinding stone. With a swirling motion she moves it in circles, beginning at the top right-hand corner of the stone and moving diagonally across to the lower left. To mix her black, she grinds both of the dark rocks, one at a time, then adds a few strokes of dried *guaco* cake and more water. The proper consistency is very important: too thin, and the color will burn out or lighten too much in the fire, and it may run during application; too thick, and the fired color my bubble or flake off.

The rutile silt is mixed with water, and if possible kept permanently in the same bowl; it is allowed to dry between painting sessions and moistened again when it is needed. The ladies maintain that in this way the material constantly improves, for easier application.

Some potters use a pencil first, to outline or to plan segments. Lucy used to use the charcoal from the wood stove or the adobe bread oven, and she still prefers it. She does make sketchy marks on the polished white pot, for certain designs—especially the complicated zigzag pattern or the rainbows coordinating the parrot designs—but I observed that she seldom bothers to follow the marks. When I asked why, she said that was just practice.

Lucy's painting touches the same quality of perfection that is seen in every aspect of her pottery. This is all the more remarkable because of the type of brush she uses: the midrib of a yucca leaf, cut into stubs and chewed until supple. Brushes are made the same way at San Ildefonso (this process is also documented in my book on Maria Martinez). When the end is soft enough, Lucy trims it to a point or straight across, and if necessary shaves it narrower. New brushes are needed all the time. It is not uncommon to see Lucy or one of the other women painting with one brush and chewing the next at the same time.

Lucy recalls sitting on the floor to paint in the old house on the mesa, with the kerosene lamp beside her; in that position more light is available from the lamp than if she sat next to it at the table. Such lantern light is not very good, and if a pot is big, it is better to wait for daylight. I find it difficult to imagine Lucy painting one hundred little pots for the tourist trade, as she says she did in the old days, in a single day.

Sometimes the women paint at Emma's, as they are doing today. Painting is tedious and exacting work. The potters liven it by visiting each other, for a change of venue—almost like quilting socials. For several days the three have been working in Emma's kitchen on the big jars Lucy has made for Houston. At least her pots are given occasional recognition now, a far cry from making hundreds of little pots, each with a different motif, to be sold for a nickel or a dime!

Lucy's pieces for the approaching exhibitions are large and would have taken her months to complete alone. Emma and Dolores have helped make the clay, rolled coils for the building, and now they are helping to paint. Even so, this is almost constant work from early morning until dusk, on many days during the autumn months.

Lucy works on the largest pot, a jar with bold black zigzags. Dolores is filling in the deer Lucy has outlined on a lidded jar. Emma fills in another zigzag design Lucy has outlined. The girls do not know how to do fine-line decoration, Lucy's specialty; that incredibly complicated geometric pattern Lucy does all by herself. Without warning, Lucy's short yucca brush, laden with black pigment, slips out of her hand. She has been holding the tall jar sideways on her left arm, like a violin, and the brush lands on the white pot, spattering it from top to bottom. The three women take turns all afternoon, scraping the black off the white background and away from the zigzag motif with a tiny jackknife.

Lucy turns to a fatter shape, an olla, already penciled with her exotic birds. A rainbow curves over the entire pot. Lucy begins the rainbow first, with the "yellow paint," which will be bright orange when fired. The rhythm here is different; unlike the geometric patterns, the flowers and parrots are painted in an exciting free fashion. This pot will bring as much money as a fine-line piece, but Lucy will finish it faster and with more joy.

There is a painting stance: body rigid, the pot held gently. The thumb and first finger hold the stub of the three-inch yucca brush hard enough to whiten the knuckles. Muscles are stiff; the arm moves only from the shoulder. Sometimes the tip of the little finger can drop to the pot, steadying the movement. The brush is dipped in pigment for every stroke. The tip goes down against the pot; the arm pulls the brush line; the hand lifts. Repeat—and repeat again: the short brush cannot hold much color, so the strokes are short. Lucy plans the stops and starts, moving the brush in the air when there is no pencil sketch on the pot; and her rhythm flows.

As the three women work at this kitchen table, six of Emma's grandchildren play nearby or pull at her, making requests. A new baby peers seriously from his cradleboard. Kittens surround their feet, wanting food. More children enter, home from school. These little ones carry textbooks written in phonetic Keresan, part of the program to teach them their own language. The noise increases, pull-toys and television adding to it. The children are well behaved, but all my senses cry out that the precision involved in this painting needs the quiet that allows intense concentration. Or am I missing something? Lucy relaxes, laughing and talking with them. She pulls a child onto her lap and bounces her knee, reveling in this chance to be young. Then she returns to the parrot pot.

How these ladies make pots says something of great importance to me, but it is something that did not become clear until I sat down and started writing. It is perhaps one of the basic reasons I undertook to write about Maria Martinez and why I have undertaken this book. As a studio potter and teacher, I have had much experience in potteries, workshops, studios, and classrooms. Such places are as familiar to me as my own skin. Yet, here are people who make pots in a place different from where such work is conventionally done. In every sense, these Indian ladies make pots in the midst of their lives. They make pots in and from Life!

Lucy dresses up to paint. Today she has on a bright orange-pink print, made Acoma-style with full wide sleeves, trimmed with lace to match the lace on the petticoat. The pink of her apron dances with the turquoise jewelry she loves to wear. Occasionally she changes clothes again for the same sitting. The women buy material for themselves wherever they travel, and gratefully accept all gifts. Everyone sews. Lucy has many pretty clothes, befitting her sunny personality, and painting time is a good chance to wear them.

In the 1930s Lucy worked with the traditional patterns of her village. The women of this pueblo had always made pots; they are necessary elements of the kiva. Lucy would have seen older pots in the kiva; later in her life she was exposed to museum collections. Acoma women also made storage jars and water pots with decorations indigenous to the pueblo. This, and the fine-line patterns on collected shards, were Lucy's rich heritage. Then, when she saw Mimbres, Mesa Verde, Chaco Canyon, and other black-on-white pottery, those designs in a sense, were already hers.

One day I took Lucy to the School for American Research in Santa Fe, to see one of the largest collections of historic period Acoma pottery. Lucy was astonished to see the immense collection of old pots on the shelves in the archives. Among these hundreds of pots she found about fifteen unsigned pieces that she had made before 1950.

Lucy's patterns now are her own innovations. "The quality of pots at Acoma today is far superior to what it used to be," says Edna Norton, an Albuquerque authority. "The painting is as beautiful as it always was, and today there are about six real potters there; Lucy is best of her generation, and was the best from the beginning. I don't know of anyone else who had that much original talent, although she never believed she had. She has indomitable spirit."

"I encourge all the Acoma to keep the hand techniques," Edna continues: "No potter's wheel, no commercial slip casting, no store-bought or mail-order colors, no electric kiln firing. If I know it isn't natural and traditional I won't buy it."

Lucy credits Katie Noe, the Gallup dealer, with giving her the idea for the heart-line deer design, which has become as much a hallmark of her work as her fine-line decoration. Miss Noe, who claims to be the only person living who was working with native American craftsmen in the 1920s, says there was a great deal of controversy in the marketplace about Lucy's deer pattern.

Lucy's first pieces for Miss Noe, in any case, included the heart-line deer, but the background was covered with all the rosettes and geometrics traditional to Acoma pots. "It took seven or eight pieces to make Lucy do it plain," she recounts. "I didn't have a picture or anything to show her, no sketch, so we just talked about it, and I kept asking her to leave things off. Finally I said to leave the background absolutely plain. Eventually she brought me one all white with just the deer nicely located, saying:

'There's nothing on it, Katie—nothing but the deer.' She was unhappy about it then, but soon it dawned on her creative mind that it was one of the best things she had ever done, and she used the principle in other ways."

Lucy changed the deer design over the years, painting it in boarders, in horizontal repeats, and starkly alone, in varying scale. From the use of the heart-line deer against the polished white ground, she proceeded to highlight other design elements by using them in isolation. A plain white background with black geometrics cascading down from the lip of the piece has been one of Lucy's real innovations as an artist—astonishing in its contrast to the patchwork quilt surfaces of most historic period Acoma pots.

FINE-LINE DECORATION

I had asked specifically to watch a large pot being painted with Lucy's famous fine-line decoration. The next time I arrived she had made two olla shapes, each about twelve inches high and nearly as wide, in case one should break during the process. The pots—white slip applied, polished, and shimmering in the sunlight—greeted me as I walked in the door. Lucy was waiting.

The day before she had blocked off one pot with a penciled grid of horizontal and vertical lines, covering the surface with rectangles about $1\frac{1}{2}$ by $2\frac{1}{2}$ inches in size. The design ended with a horizontal line drawn about two inches up from the bottom of the piece. Lucy makes pencil marks entirely freehand, without any measuring instrument, and preparing these two pieces was a full day's work.

This morning before breakfast, still in her bedclothes, Lucy gathers the paint grinding stone, water, several pigment rocks to make more pigment, the pot, and a short yucca brush. The first step is to wet the brown iron pigment already on the metate. It is not enough, so Dolores adds to it by grinding the rocks, one an iron-oxide rust color, the other a brown-black manganese dioxide color. To this she adds dried *guaco*, grinding the tar-black chunk against the stone and into the mixture. She judges the color and texture of the pigment from long experience of working with her mother.

Lucy moistens the end of the yucca brush with the pigment and bands the top with two lines, turning the pot with her left hand on the oilcloth-covered table and painting with a smooth motion. She stops every few inches to rewet the brush. Then, holding the pot sideways in her lap, she chooses one of the top group of rectangles, outlining it with pigment.

The fine-line decoration is a carnival of optical effects. Lucy first saw the patterns of close black lines on old pot shards she gathered when she was a little girl; the shards still fascinate her after all these years, and, when she has a spare moment, which is not often, she goes out to search for them. Her own designs for pottery when she was young were the traditional orange, brown, and black bird-and-flower patterns. Gradually she began to experiment with fine black lines in her own work. Later she saw the work of her Anasazi ancestors, who created their astonishing designs from about the eighth to the thirteenth centuries.

When she began to adapt the fine-line decoration, she had to decide how to expand the motifs on pot fragments to large, three-dimensional forms. Her first efforts were merely single lines girdling pots; eventually she developed the repeat pattern of fine lines forming the illusion of a star. In the 1940s, after she had perfected this, she worked out variations: wide, solid black zigzags, zigzag outlines filled in with fine hatching, and fine-line patterns covering asymmetric areas.

The blue ribbon Lucy won at the 1950 Gallup Intertribal Ceremonial, her first competitive exhibition, was for a large, fine-line water jar. Some years later, her work came to the attention of Kenneth Chapman of the Laboratory of Anthropology, who began to show her the pots in the museum collection. This was her artistic heritage, and she consumed it whole, immeasurably excited in her own quiet way. She still experiments with variations on the fine-line and black diagonal zigzag patterns. Her daughters still bring her pictures and books when they find them, but these are no longer necessary; Lucy has the work of her ancestors in her body and heart and mind.

"Some folks," notes Dolores, "say Lucy couldn't be painting this fine-line design today, that she's too old. But Lucy can hold the yucca brush better than any of us younger potters—and stay at it longer, too." Lucy smiles.

Lucy outlines the first rectangle, then begins her pattern by drawing three closely spaced diagonals from the lower left corner to the upper right. Next, she makes two diagonals from the top left corner to the center lines, and two more from the center to the lower right corner, dividing the rectangle in quarters. Into each space she puts a triangle, one short line at a time, wetting the brush before each stroke. Each triangle is filled in with fine concentric triangles. She moves right, then left, then left, and right again. She pulls the pattern freely, without any previously penciled lines, holding the short stub of the brush between thumb and first finger. Her wrist is absolutely steady making the line, and the pot is turned slightly each time for the next stroke. This patience and control are prodigious.

Lucy's youngest child—her seventh daughter—has come to join the painting session, bringing her own small pots but using her mother's pigment. Dolores is also in the group now, with a few of her pots that need 'touching up' from the last firing. They hold the fragile raw pots carefully, dipping the yucca brush into the liquid color after each stroke, over and over.

The pigment has dried on its grinding stone. Dolores rubs the black rock, then the iron-red rock, back and forth against the grinding stone, adding tiny amounts of water periodically, then grinding in some of the dried *guaco*. "If you get too much of any one of these, the color will flake and fall off, or it will dust off after the firing," she explains. "You have to get just the right mix. There's no way to measure except how many times you rub against the stone, and sometimes I don't count." In fact, I have seen Dolores rigorously count the strokes for each pigment.

Each of these women has her own small pan of tools, including polishing stones, awls, pieces of chamois, gourd tools, and metal scraping lids; many of these are hand-me-downs. Some tools are communal and can be shared. Brushes are made on the spot, when they are needed; everyone keeps a yucca stalk with leaves close by for the purpose. Perhaps the most precious of these tools is the pigment grinding stone, usually an old metate found in a field or given by a relative who previously used it for corn or wheat. "We all care about our paint grinding stones," says Dolores. "You can't make paint without your own paint stone, and you can't mix on anybody else's. Everybody rubs in a different way, and each metate knows its owner."

It has taken Lucy all morning to paint six fine-line rectangles, and there are perhaps fifty more to go. She sets the pot slowly on the table and turns it gently; she seems pleased with the results so far. Then she rises and withdraws to the back part of the house to rest for about thirty minutes. When she returns, she has changed into finery: her sky-blue dress with the yellow orchid print, made of fabric brought to her from Hawaii; her crochet-trimmed apron; a turquoise manta pin on her breast; a large squash blossom necklace, earrings, bracelets, and rings—all of turquoise; a small red Hopi sash on her braid. Emma, who has dropped by for a short visit, stands up to comb her mother's hair.

This is the last day I will be here to photograph her—the manuscript is due in a few weeks—and this morning we have again thumbed through my book on Maria Martinez together. Lucy must have decided that she wanted to appear in print in her brightest things.

Emma picks up a corner of Lucy's apron to examine the crocheted lace trim and begins to reminisce about the crocheting that Lucy used to do. "She had patterns, and she would follow even the most complicated ones—you know, the ones with all the fine threads. Maybe it had something to do with her fine-line painting. I used to kneel there beside her, watching how she pulled the needle with all the different threads. She was so fast! I could only learn how to make the chain. She taught me to embroider, too, but I only did the cross-stitch; she did everything."

Lucy sits down again at the table, picks up her pot, and begins another rectangle. When two black lines occasionally merge, she uses the awl to scrape back to the polished white. In two days, twelve rectangles are outlined and filled in. The pot will take perhaps two more weeks to finish.

She has been painting this decoration on various shapes for more than forty years, and these pots are her most famous. It is difficult to imagine how she first developed this intricate pattern. The pots are chillingly perfect. Even more spectacular, to my mind, are the pieces that developed from the allover fine-line pattern: some show a minimum of black decoration placed artfully on the polished white background; others are zigzag patterns, winding circuitous ways around different pot forms. Sometimes she uses an angular pattern of outlines and forms filled in with fine lines. These are the innovations that have emerged and evolved over the years, as her creative imagination grew.

Why does Lucy make pots? What is the impetus or impulse behind her potting?

Again, where do Lucy's pots come from? These may seem like silly questions with self-evident answers, but the answers are important and are not all obvious at first glance. Financial considerations naturally are present, but these are not fundamental. The price of a pot does not enter into its making. The movements of the marketplace, in particular, have no bearing. Lucy once made ashtrays that sold for a few pennies. The purpose of the ashtrays was to meet financial need; the purposes of pots today may be an exhibition, a commission, an Indian market, or perhaps a grandchild's hospital bill. And each pot partakes of something that has value beyond price. Lucy knows this. It is as if she—her incomparable skill—was the instrument of something vast and ancient and alive. Lucy works joyously, always a little surprised at the result—at the varieties of form and style and decoration she has achieved even within the same group of pieces.

Each piece is considered several times during its progress, initially for form and whether or not to add more, then for refinement and polish, and finally for the decoration most suitable for the form. Designs on the flat are quite different in the round, and the forms of Lucy's pieces decide the way in which familiar patterns will be worked and adjusted. When she is contemplating a new design, her concentration is deep; she may sit for hours looking at the shape of the pot in all its nuances, under the light and in the shadow at dusk. I have watched some thirty large and an equal number of small works formed, scraped, water-smoothed, slipped, polished, and decorated this autumn. Each piece has its own life and vitality. The Acoma say that each pot has a spirit.

FIRING

Some pots Lucy made three weeks ago are dry now and ready to be fired. We are at Emma's house for firing day, and down by the old bread oven Emma's and Dolores's sons have been preparing the coals. This is the first sunny day in a week; there is no wind. The firing area is a flat spot of ground near the road, next to the old adobe house Toribio built when he moved his family from McCartys village. The ground is still wet from the cold weather, but for several hours a fire has been blazing, to dry the surface. The ladies are making this firing attempt for me; ordinarily they would not risk the dampness, which may cause reduction to occur in the firing, resulting in smoke-spots on the polished white ware.

Since we have to wait for the ground to dry, the women are hoping to have more pieces to fire. Boxes of pots ready for decoration were brought this morning from Dolores's house to Emma's. The pieces Lucy had worked on the week before on the mesa are also here. On the table, Lucy lines up four not quite finished pots and looks at them. She picks the lid off one and touches a spot with her brush, puts the lid back and looks again. When she is satisfied, the pots are packed in dish towels in a basket to carry to the fire.

Other boxes and washtubs full of pots are already waiting below, along with a bucket full of big shards—the remains of pots that broke or exploded in previous firings, which will be used to shield the new ware. Emma's and Dolores' sons are helping today; one of the boys comes up to the house to say that everything is ready.

We walk to the kiln site together, through the corn and melon field. The field is full of melons left on the vine, because everyone had tired of eating them.

An area ten feet in diameter has been prepared, and the wood reduced to piles of ash. Lucy bends over with a stick, leveling the ash. The boys disappear into the old house and return with bushel baskets of dried cow chips. The women lay a flat layer of dried dung over the ash; over that they place a layer of shards. These shards are rearranged many times to make just the right base. The pots are placed over the shard layer, and another layer of shards covers the pots, then a new row of pots is stacked on top of these shards. Rows of pots and shards alternate, until all the pots have been stacked. A layer of shards covers the top. The entire structure resembles a dome in shape.

Big cow chips are placed on edge around the circle of shards and pots, as the construction continues. The bucket of shards is a history in fragments of Lucy's potting career: bits of heart-line deer, fine-line, parrots, feather designs, and flute players, bottoms of broken pots—some with Lucy's signature.

Lucy helps to build the kiln. The ladies chatter as they work, changing, fitting and maneuvering the pots and shards so that they do not touch each other except at minute points, where unavoidable. An excitement gradually increases. Open spaces must be allowed in and around the stacked pots for the circulation of air. These white pots with yellow and orange decorations need an even, oxidizing atmosphere.

As soon as the last shards go on and the arrangement is satisfactory, the dome is covered with the last layer of cow chips. Each of the three women quietly takes a pinch of cornmeal from an apron or out of a pocket to sprinkle on the ground in prayer.

We wad pages of newspaper and collect twigs in the field, until we have enough to begin the fire. These are piled around the base of the dung dome and stuck in among the cow chips. Arms folded, Lucy watches the sky to gauge the weather for the next few hours; Dolores and Emma light paper torches and ignite the kiln as fast as possible all around the circumference.

We stand mesmerized by the flames, watching them swirl upwards; suddenly the flames bend, indicating a wind has started, though we do not feel it. If wind is allowed to blow through the pots, the firing will be uneven in temperature and so will be the color of the pots. The ladies hurry to build a six-foot wind shield of wood and metal scraps a few feet from the kiln. Ash from the bonfire is shoveled around the base to further insure that the wind does not blow up through the kiln.

Trucks pass on the freeway and on the old Highway 66, drivers honking and waving. Both roads are a stone's throw away. The women say that this always happens when they are firing or baking bread; some drivers stop to see what is going on and stay to watch the finished pottery removed. "We've made a lot of friends this way," they laugh.

The fire is burning well; even a few feet away the heat is intense. Some smoke rises—a bad omen. The women take their poking sticks and gingerly move cow chips around until the smoke is eliminated and the fire once again burns clean. The pots will mature from the heat of the smoldering manure; the wood ignited at the beginning around the base was only to start the chips.

This firing is noticeably different from those for black or red ware at San Ildefonso and Santa Clara, which burn much longer, stronger, and hotter. The temperature must be higher for the carbon deposition that yields the jet-black pots. Red ware, too, demands more heat to enrich the color.

Firing at Hopi pueblos is done with the dung of deer, squirrel, or rabbit, at temperatures hardly hotter than a hot oven. There the look of the ware implies a mixed atmosphere—clean to smoky, oxidizing to reducing—causing wonderful color changes. The kiln is piled loosely, with plenty of air vents, which also means that its heat retention is poor. The Acoma firing fits between the Hopi and San Ildefonso temperatures.

It should be pointed out that an open bonfire or dung fire does not reach a temperature of more than 1300°F or so. Clays require a firing temperature of over 2000°F to be durable. The Pueblo peoples made their pottery for use, with the certainty that new pots would replace broken ones. For collectors, however, if preservation is an aim, care must be exercised not to chip or scratch the fragile wares or to subject them to moisture. For cleaning, only a dry, soft cloth should be used.

We began building the kiln at noon, and so far an hour has passed; I am about to learn another difference between the firing for black ware and this one for white ware. The girls say we can leave it alone until it is finished. What? No kiln should be left unwatched, I thought. San Ildefonso's firing, for example, must be watched constantly. But no, the women are already moving away. It is time for lunch.

We walk up the rain-washed and deeply grooved dirt road to Emma's. Lucy excuses herself to lie down, and Emma starts to make tortillas. For this batch she uses four hands of flour mixed with lard dipped up with the fingertips of one hand, the same amount of baking powder, and a few pinches of local salt. Enough warm water is added to make a pliable dough, which is then kneaded. A stew of meat and potatoes with red chili has been on the stove all morning. Dolores has brought a bag of green chilis to roast and peel. Emma adds these to another stew of leftover corn and meat. Bowls and spoons are set on the table, and soon the food is ready.

Impatient, I go to look at the firing before lunch. One hour and a half has passed since we went down to stack the pots. Some of the dung has burned completely down to a white ash, cow chips have fallen inward, and some shards at the top are exposed; the chips still standing are carbon black or gray. The firing is, in fact, finished—in less than forty-five minutes. The pieces will remain in the kiln for some hours yet, but ostensibly the caved-in hole is cooling the ware.

When I return to the house, I find that Emma has added blue corn porridge, tea made from some wild herb, and watermelon from the fields. The conversation turns to Lucy's forthcoming exhibition in Houston and the award that she is to receive there. It is time to choose the pots and price them. I have been wondering what value Lucy would put on certain pieces; this is never decided until after the firing, the results of which are always uncertain.

And I wonder, for the millionth time perhaps, how do I, how do we, value a pot? Besides physical and technical considerations, besides "artistry," there is a whole world of intangible values. Edna Norton says that she has always believed that just holding an Indian pot makes you feel better. She relates that one day a man came into her shop, looking at the prices of the relatively expensive pots. After conversing a bit with him, she thrust a pot into his hands. "How does it feel?" she asked. "Good," he replied. "Buy it," she said, and the man did. Several days later he came back and told Edna, "It worked." "What?" she asked. "You told me to buy a pot because it felt good. Well, holding it still makes me feel good. I am a psychiatrist, and I've started to send other people out to buy Indian pots to make them feel better."

Some of Lucy's pieces bring hundreds of dollars today, but she only makes a few pots for sale each year. This autumn, her output is far greater than usual due to two exhibitions. We have witnessed an outpouring. Each vessel is unique; each vessel sings.

The best way to buy an Indian pot is directly from the potter, at the pueblo or at a fair. Dealers sometimes take unfair advantage of both the Indian artists and the customer. Lucy and her daughters have the opportunity to meet a lot of people when they teach in the summer at Idyllwild School of Music and the Arts, in California, and do demonstrations in various places. Conversely, many people, including potential customers, have the opportunity to get to know these ladies. Pottery is the only means of livelihood for many Pueblo people, and it should be remembered that some women potters are the sole means of support for extended families.

No one is really keeping time, but it seems long enough. The pots should be ready. We all walk down to the firing site. The kiln has burned down to half the size it was when we began. The cow chips have so disintegrated that much of the pottery is bare in the ashes. Wearing gloves, Emma and Dolores shovel away the remaining dung and ash and begin to pick up the hot pots; Lucy has remained in the house.

Everything is whole; nothing is chipped or cracked. Dolores points out a scratch on one deer painting and explains that this happens when the dung falls on a piece during the firing. Emma picks up Lucy's lidded pot, turns it over and exclaims: "Oh, see the transfer!" A shard will occasionally "transfer" to a pot, meaning that the action of the flame or smoke will mark the outline of a shard on a pot surface. And there are a few "smoke clouds," puffs of gray visible on the white background.

In some places the polished white slip takes on an allover gray or cream-colored cast. This has to do with the way the pots and shards are stacked, with the amount of cow chips burned, with the humidity or lack of it, with the number of pots fired, and with the amount of paper and wood used at the start. So much more can go wrong with a simple kiln of this kind than with a commercial or industrial kiln; the difficulties are great, and an enormous amount of technique—which comes from the accumulation of experience—is involved. The simplest materials and processes can be the most demanding. This is perhaps the defining characteristic of native American pottery.

I find the slight color changes charming, but the women disagree; the dealers, they say, are buying only the most perfectly white pots. This is not Lucy's worry, as she seldom fails to sell everything she makes directly to personal customers, but her children occasionally still sell through middlemen. The demand for "unblemished" work denies the richness that is intrinsic to this kind of firing and this pottery. The way to produce sterile, standard, uniform ware is to fire in an electric kiln, where no smoke can "mar" the pots—and many potters are secretly doing this.

Some Acoma potters are even buying greenware from the hobby shops. Some paint with commercial ceramic colors rather than natural earth pigments. And some are using a clear glaze over the painting. "Most people don't know the difference," Emma contends. "Even at Indian Market we have seen prizes go to this kind of pot. They don't get jurors who are knowledgeable. We wish Indian Market would stick to its rules about real traditional craft; we wish dealers would care about the outdoor firing, and especially about the pottery being handmade of our own clay."

"I used to think you really had to be absolutely traditional in the firing," says dealer Katie Noe. "But today I don't think the new dealers know the difference. The old dealers are in their seventies and eighties; we know how it was. Today the ladies of Acoma need money for their families—more now than they used to. The dung-chip firing breaks pots, makes blemishes, causes smoke spots. Many dealers don't like that, and more important, they have trained the ladies not to like those things either.

The traditional firing I saw was done under pressure, for the fast-approaching exhibitions of Lucy's work. Ordinarily, pottery is made slowly; clay sieving and mixing, making, scraping, water-smoothing, polishing, and decorating—all demand skill and concentration and should not be hurried. For the past few months, Emma and Dolores have been helping their mother scrape, polish, and decorate, because of the exhibition demands. Firing should wait for the right day, the right ground, the right stillness in the air for oxidation.

Even so, there is always speculation. Will this pot be all right? Will the lid still fit after the firing? Will the surface be unblemished? To my eye, smoke marks, a measure of gray in the whiteness, a darker yellow or orange from the titanium and uranium pigments, all make for interest and vitality.

The mellowness of the vessels from this cow chip firing has delighted the women. They sit at the table fondling the pots, hands lightly feeling the surface, pointing to an especially fine painting, quietly examining with grateful pride. The matriarch watches her two daughters. She seems to be casting a silent challenge for them to grasp her own vigor, and to carry on from that wellspring.

From the beginning Lucy was imbued with something extraordinary—an energy, an artistic impulse, a penetrating sense, and an exuberance, as well as great skill. Her pots are personal visions. Seeing them, we sense something of the power of this extraordinary woman who, quietly and alone, dissolved the restraints of her society and found her individual vision. This in itself was unprecedented and revolutionary.

Some of Lucy's pieces will be part of pueblo life. Set in the context of pueblo tradition, they fit. Set in the context of a visionary contemporary art idiom, they almost overwhelm.

Unheralded, strong artists may arise within a communal art to speak to us all. They are not individualists in our narrow sense. They are part of something much bigger—something we call a tradition—and they use this power to become giants. It was the function of the visionary, the see-er, the shaman, to be an intermediary between the sacred and the everyday, to put something of the sacred into everyday life. Such, traditionally, has been the role of the Pueblo artist, who, given permission by the community, uses independent energies unconsciously to effect beauty that lasts.

Where do we go from here? That this question has no answer breaks our hearts. Maria and the few others like her are dead. When Lucy goes, there is no one to fill her place—yet. Still, her vitality imbues her objects with an authority, a kind of tradition. Lucy's work contains the play of grand forces. The prehistoric legacy, the history, her own revolt and self-insistence communicate in spite of everything, in spite of Lucy herself, and will command followers. The power of Lucy Lewis's pots is absolute, quite mysteriously absolute.

You and I, we like the marks of fire. But I don't fight about electric kiln firings: it's a losing battle."

156. The clay is brought from the secret place in large chunks and pounded into gravel-like bits. A grinding machine is then used to pulverize it.   157–59. Emma adds water to the mixture of powdered clay and finely ground shards then kneads the clay into a plastic mass.   160. She pats the clay into balls then mashes these balls into a mass again for storage in a plastic bag.

161, 162. Dolores mixes clay by adding water until it is the consistency of cream. This thick slip is screened through a nylon mesh curtain. 163–65. It is then poured into cookie sheets, dried, ground on a metate, then mixed with water and foot-wedged until plastic. Both Emma and Dolores prepare the clay their mother uses.

163. Acoma clay before it is ground.   164. Belle's son helps wedge the clay.   165.
Dolores foot-wedges her clay into plasticity.   166 (*facing page*). Lucy closes the
top of a seed pot with quick movements of the gourd tool.

Seed Pot

167–69. A seed pot begins with a form pinched from a ball. Lucy rolls a long coil and attaches it to the form in the *huditzi*. **170, 171.** The form is raised and thinned by adding coils then lifting up with the action of a gourd tool while pressing out from the inside. It is then expanded to fill the *huditzi* and formed into a pumpkin-like shape.

172–74. Each coil is attached by finger-pressing it all the way around then repeating the process in the opposite direction. More coils are added to bring the curve inward. The gourd tool is used to pull the clay and reduce the size of the pot mouth.   175. The piece is taken out of the *huditzi* for finishing.   176. Lucy has worked half a day and she rests.

MINIATURES

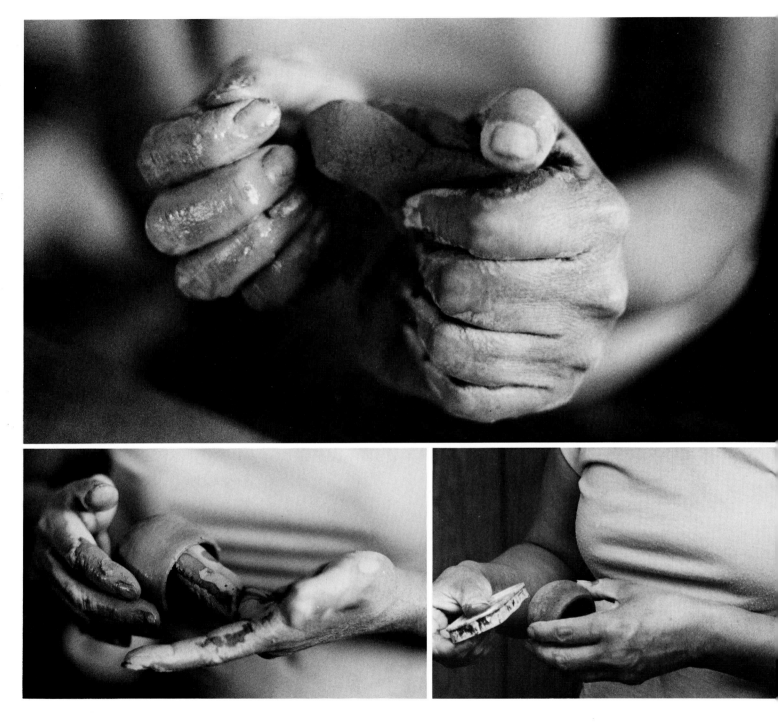

177. Emma kneads the clay for a miniature pot.   178. Fingers shape and smooth the tiny pot.   179. The miniature is scraped prior to being water-smoothed.

180. Lucy touches up a miniature pot.

181, 182. A first coil is added to the rough bowl form in a *huditzi*, and the form is raised by smoothing the inside with a gourd tool.

183. Two more coils have been added, the form transferred to a larger *huditzi*, then rounded and shaped with a gourd tool. The surface is kept wet. **184, 185.** After the form has been further expanded and refined, it is removed from the *huditzi*. With a gourd tool, Lucy indents the top of the form and gradually increases this convex curve. **186** (*facing page*). Lucy fists out a rough shape before putting it into the *huditzi*.

187. Lucy paddles the bottom to achieve a round, symmetrical form.   188. The pot is ready to be water-smoothed and the lip trimmed.   189. Holding the pot in one hand, Lucy trims the pot lip straight and true with a knife.

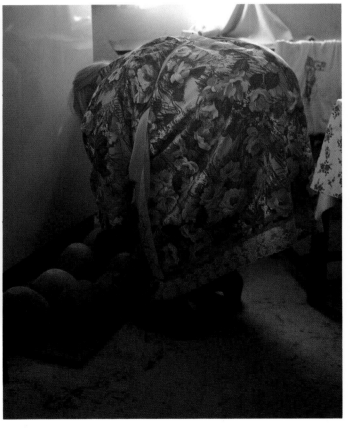

190, 191. Lucy refines the forms of a group of water jars. The jars are stored upside down, waiting to be slipped and polished.

192. Emma often works in her kitchen, amid a bustle of children and grandchildren. Her bowl and plate forms offer generous surfaces for her Mimbres-inspired designs.   193. Dolores is best known for her small pots and canteens decorated with traditional geometric patterns. Here she helps texture her mother's corrugated pot. 194, 195. Andrew, living and working in the family house on the mesa, is concerned with very large jar forms.

196. Emma makes pottery quietly in her kitchen.   197, 198. Children take care of each
other while the women are busy with pottery.

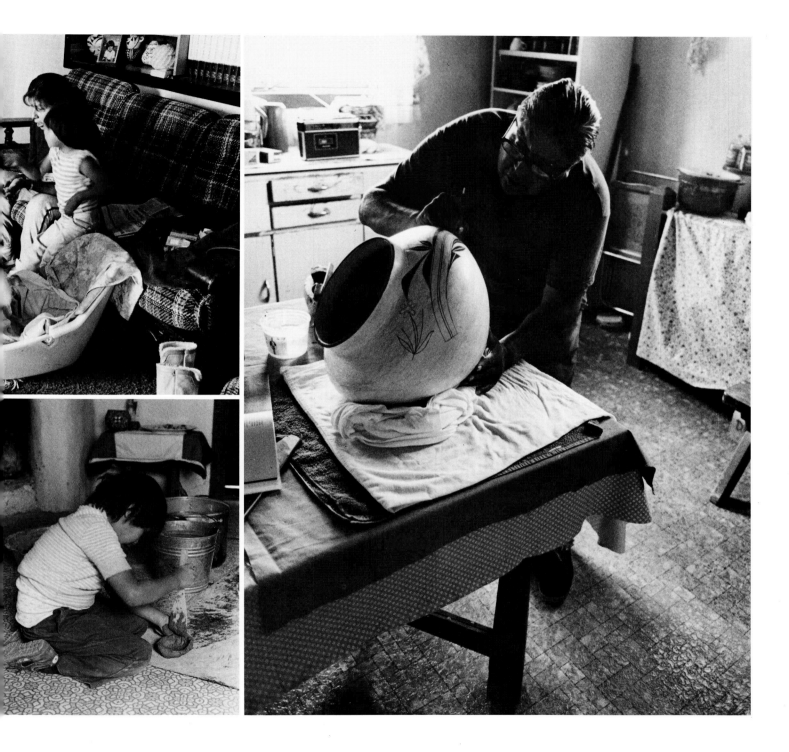

199. Pottery-making is a part of life for everyone in the family. **200.** Andrew Lewis paints a large water jar.

Large Jar

201. Lucy's tools.   **202.** The primal, rough form in a *huditzi* gives no indication of size of the pot being made.

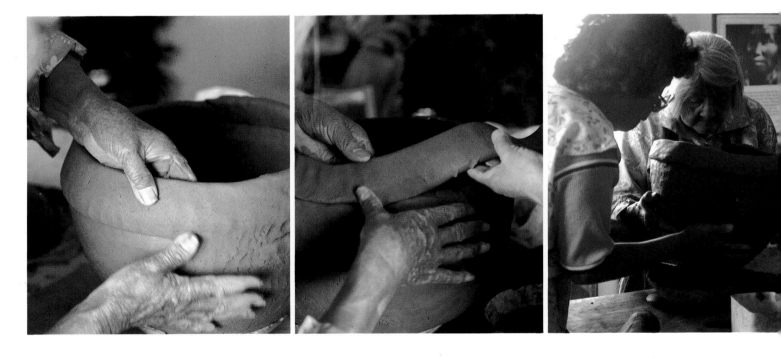

203–05. Dolores makes large, flat coils and helps hold them, freeing Lucy to concentrate on the joining.   **206.** As the form becomes larger, it is moved to a second, more capacious *huditzi*. The flat coils are angled inward to reduce the diameter of the pot.   **207.** Dolores helps Lucy lift the pot into a third *huditzi*.   **208.** The inside and outside have been smoothed, and another coil is added.

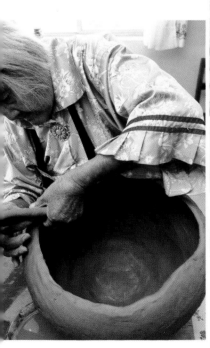

210. Weight and size cause the pot form to sag dangerously.   211. Carefully the pot is lifted in a dish towel into a large wooden bowl.   212. More coils have been added to enlarge and curve the form.   213. After twenty-four hours, the pot is stiff enough to indent a reverse curve.   214. The ragged lip is cut and smoothed.   215. Lucy constantly refines the form and smooths the lip with her fingers.   216. The inverted form is paddled to achieve symmetry and to indent the base.   217. Small pieces of clay are used to fill any cracks.

CORRUGATED POT

218-20. Lucy takes a small amount of clay to begin the coil that will form the spiral bottom of a corrugated pot.

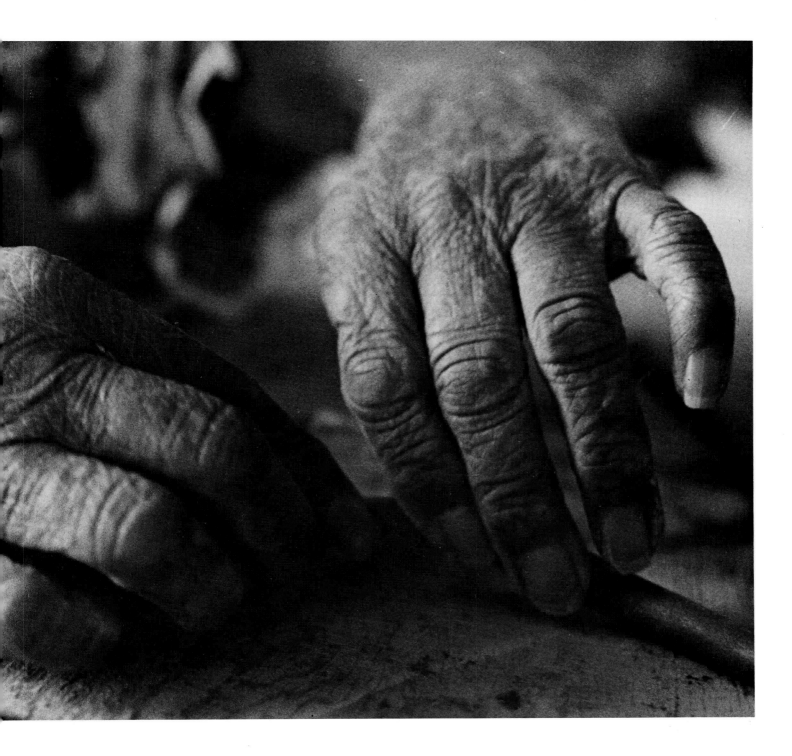

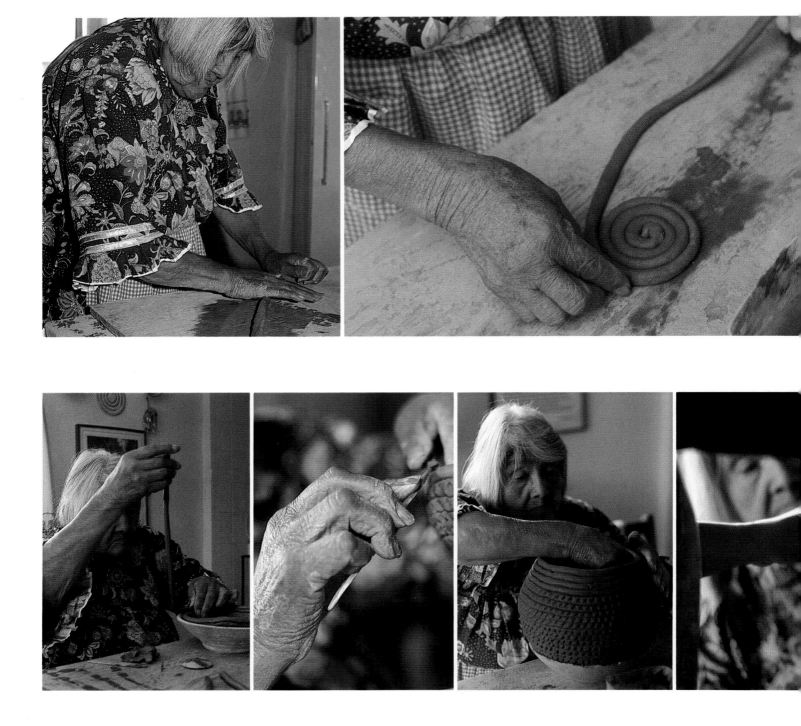

221, 222. Lucy rolls a long, thin coil and forms a spiral for the bottom.   223, 224. The interior of the base is smoothed with a gourd tool, and the outside surface is textured with a special, carved cedar stick.   225. The bottom is widened with more coils, smoothed, textured, then put in a *huditzi*.   226. Coils are impressed with the cedar tool.   227. More of the thin coils are added to make the form taller, the interior is smoothed with a gourd tool, and the exterior coils are textured.   228. Each coil is placed on the inside edge of the previous one to bring in the form.

230–32. The lip is cut and smoothed. The wooden tool has been carved to make a decorative impression, which enrichens the textured effect.

233–35. Dolores scrapes a pot then smoothes it with water and a stone. **236.** A bowl of scrapings shows how carefully clay is conserved. These will be mixed into the next batch of fresh clay. The small pot has been water-smoothed.

237. The pebble for smoothing is wet before using. 238, 239. Lucy develops a smooth surface with water and a pebble or with her fingers. 240. White clay (kaolin) for making slip comes in chunks. 241. It is slaked in water for some days, lumps are worked out, then it is thinned for application in several coats.

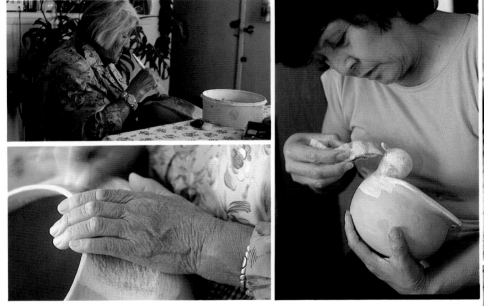

242, 243. Lucy applies white slip with a brush then polishes it with a polishing stone while the slip is still wet. Only a small area is done at one time. 244. Emma applies the slip with a rag. 245. A polished jar in front of a partly polished vessel. 246. Many of Lucy's thin-walled pots are so fragile that they break during the polishing.

247–49. Emma grinds a pigment rock with a little water. A cake of *guaco* is ground into the pigment as a binder. The pigment is mixed, and the consistency is tested with the tip of a yucca brush.

250–52. Lucy applies black pigment to the lip of the pot, slowly, as she turns it in her lap. A pigment Lucy calls "yellow paint" is used for a rainbow and parrot. **253, 254.** Holding the yucca spine brush rock steady, Lucy outlines a spike pattern. Dolores fills in patterns that Lucy outlined. In Plate 254, Lucy's penciled pattern can be glimpsed. It is clear that she did not follow it.

255(A, B). Emma chews a yucca leaf midrib to make a brush.   256. Lucy checks the complicated spike pattern she has just completed.

257. Lucy and her daughters often paint together. Here Dolores helps her mother with pots for an exhibition.

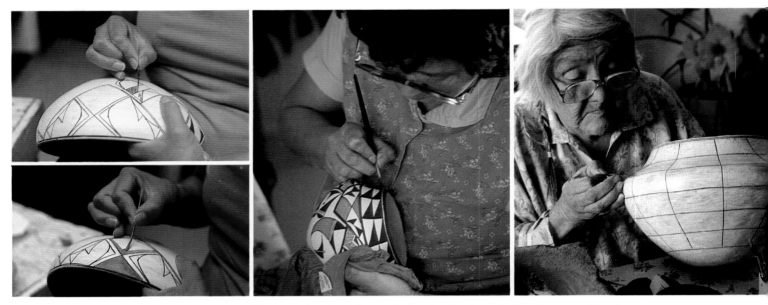

258, 259. Emma paints one of her own bowls with *guaco* and "yellow paint." 260. Dolores touches up a blemish on a finished Lucy pot before refiring. 261–63. Lucy's fine-line decoration begins with marking rectangles on the polished white surface. This took one whole day. On the second day she filled in alternate rectangles on the first and second row with the diagonals and triangles that form the "star" pattern. The pigment is hematite rock ground on a metate. 264. Lucy uses a fine awl to sharpen the edges of the black lines. 265. Andrew begins the painting of a bird-and-feather design on one of his large pots. 266. Lucy has been signing the bottoms of her pots since 1950.

267. Polished and painted pots ready for the fire. 268. Shards used to protect the vessels being fired. 269–72. The shards are carefully placed on a bed of cow chips, and Lucy brings pots and nests them in the shards. Shard and pot layers alternate, until the last pots to be fired are completely covered by shards, and the mound is covered with overlapping cow chips. 273–75. Newspaper and twigs placed around the base are ignited. Ash heaped at the base protects against drafts in the firing. The cow chips catch fire, smolder, and turn to white ash in about thirty minutes. 276. The firing is finished in about forty-five minutes, but the pots may be allowed to remain undisturbed for a few hours.

277. Lucy and Emma discuss the pots they have just fired.

278. Black-on-white jar, scroll and zigzag pattern, ca. 1940. H. 14 cm.

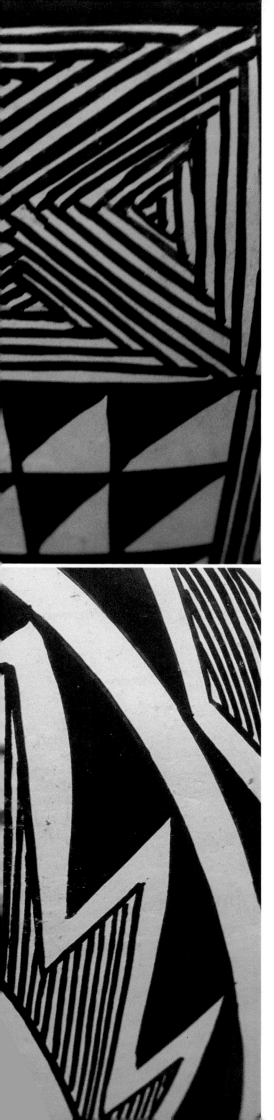

279–82. Details of Lucy's pots: unfired polychrome pot with traditional parrot design, 1983; black-on-white feather pattern and fine-line decoration, 1983; polychrome feather and braid pattern, 1960 (canteen, Plate 296); black-on-white zigzag design, 1981. **283.** Bowl, zigzag design with relief on rim, ca. 1975. D. 25 cm. **284.** Four jars, 1980. H. 10–15 cm.

285. Water jar, rainbird design, 1975. H. 15 cm.   **286.** Water jar, feather pattern, 1950. H. 20 cm.   **287.** Ceremonial jar, ca. 1950. H. 25 cm.   **288.** Wedding vase, parrot and rainbow design, 1978. H. 15 cm.

289. Water jar, parrot and rainbow design, ca. 1945. H. 15.2 cm.

290. Water jar, feather pattern and fine-line decoration, 1979. H. 15 cm. **291.** Jar, parrot and rainbow design, 1983. H. 17 cm. **292.** Pitcher, flute player design, 1950s. H. 22.5 cm. **293.** Water jar, parrot and flower design, ca. 1950. H. 22 cm. **294.** Water jar, heart-line deer design, n.d. H. 22.5 cm.

295. Food bowl, rainbird design, ca. 1925. H. 12.7 cm.

296. Ceremonial canteen, feather pattern, 1960. D. 22.5 cm.   297. Ceremonial canteen, 1960. D. 15 cm.   298. Ceremonial canteens, 1970. Right D. 15 cm.   299. Ceremonial canteen, rainbird design, n.d. D. 17 cm.   300 (*facing page*). Ceremonial canteen, parrot and feather design, 1950s. D. 17.5 cm.

301. Jar, fine-line decoration, 1950. H.
15 cm.   **302.** Jar, heart-line deer design,
1960. H. 15 cm.   **303.** Jar, spike pattern,
1960. H. 12.5 cm.

304. Jar, zigzag pattern, award winner New Mexico State Fair 1962. H. 21.2 cm.

305. Jar, spike pattern in spiral panels, 1958. H. about 25 cm. Variations of this pattern appear on three different jar shapes on this page. **306.** Seed pot, zigzag pattern, 1981. H. 17.5 cm. **307.** Jar, fine-line spike pattern in spiral panels, 1979. H. 20 cm. **308.** Seed pot, spike pattern in spiral panels, ca. 1940. H. 15 cm.

309. Water jar, fine-line decoration, 1981. H. 17.5 cm.
310 (*overleaf*). Bowl, stepped pattern, ca. 1945. D. 34.3 cm.

311. Chicken, ca. 1930. H. 12.1 cm.   312. Wedding vase, parrot and rainbow design, 1983. H. 15 cm.   313. Ash-bowl made for the tourist trade in the 1920s. D. 15 cm.   314. Lidded jar, heart-line deer design, animal lid handle, 1983. H. 22.5 cm.   315. Bowl by Emma Lewis, heart-line deer design, n.d. D. 22.5 cm. This pot is an interesting combination of tradition and personal choice and illustrates the strength of Lucy's artistic lineage.   316. Small water jar, Mimbres-inspired deer design, 1983. H. 7.5 cm.   317. Lucy was the first potter of her generation at Acoma to make miniatures.

318. Prayer-meal bowl, impressed rim, 1983. H. 10 cm.   319. Jar, scalloped lip, zigzag design (detail, Plate 282), 1983. H. 25 cm.   320. Corrugated jar and two small jars, one with Mimbres-inspired deer, 1983. H. 22.5 cm.   321. Small jar, Mimbres-inspired animals, 1983. H. 10 cm.   322. Jar, Mimbres-inspired lizard design, 1960. H. 25 cm.   323. Jar with effigy figures, n.d. H. 15 cm.

324. Bowl, black-on-white Mimbres-inspired Koshore dancer design, 1960. D. 16.3 cm.   **325.** Bowl, black-on-white Mimbres-inspired lizard design, 1960. D. 16.5 cm.   **326.** Ceremonial rattle, black-on-white, ca. 1930. L. 20 cm.

327. Polychrome wedding vase, parrot and rainbow design, 1980. H.
20 cm. 328. Pitcher, black-on-white pattern with lizard handle, 1960. H.
15.8 cm. 329. Polychrome turkey figurine, 1963. H. 10.7 cm.

330. Drum, ca. 1940. H. 15.8 cm. 331. Water jar, spiral pattern, ca. 1940. H. 24.2 cm. 332, 333. Small jars for dipping water, 1983. Both H. 10 cm.

334. Water jar, by Andrew Lewis, 1983. H. 25 cm. **335.** Jar, feather pattern, by Andrew Lewis, 1983. H. 27 cm. **336.** Water jar, parrot design, by Andrew Lewis, 1983. H. 22.5 cm. **337.** Medicine bowl, by Dolores Lewis, stepped rim, 1983. D. 15 cm.

338. Miniature plates, by Emma Lewis, 1983. D. 5 cm. 339. Canteen, Mimbres-inspired design, by Emma Lewis, 1983. H. 15 cm. 340. Plate, by Emma Lewis, n.d. D. 25 cm. 341. Miniature plates, by Emma Lewis, 1983. D. 5 cm.

342. Small ceremonial canteen, by Dolores Lewis, 1983. H. 7.5 cm.   343. Small ceremonial canteens, by Dolores Lewis, 1983. Top H. 7.5 cm.   344. Miniature wedding vase, by Dolores Lewis. H. 7.5 cm.

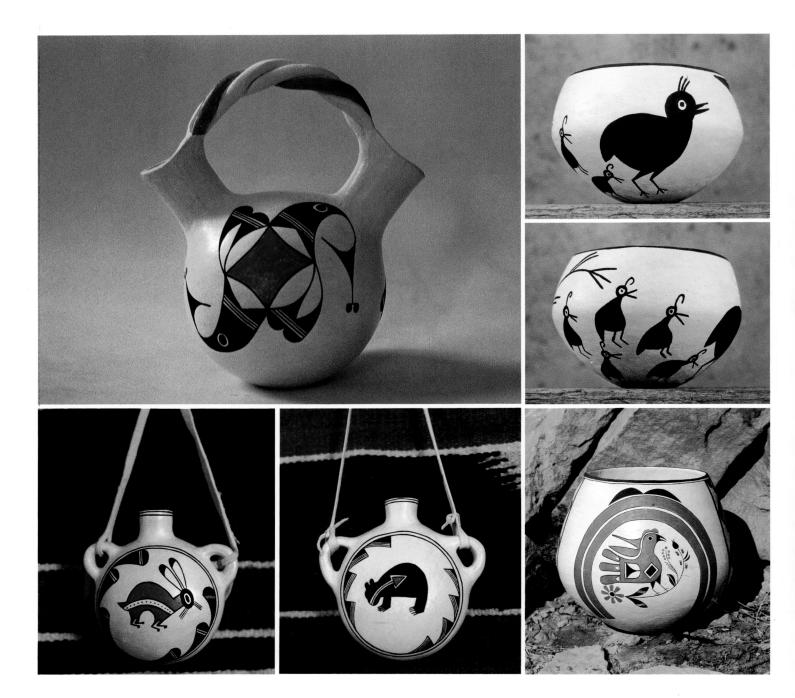

345. Wedding vase, by Dolores Lewis, rainbird design, 1979. H. 12 cm.   346, 347. Bowl, by Emma Lewis, quail design, 1983. H. 12.5 cm.   348, 349. Canteens, by Dolores Lewis, rabbit and bear designs, 1983. D. 15 cm.   350. Jar, by Emma Lewis, parrot and rainbow design, 1983. H. 20 cm.   351. Parrot effigy pot, by Emma Lewis, 1983. H. 12 cm.

LUCY'S AWARDS

LUCY HAS WON BLUE RIBBONS AND certificates constantly since she began to submit her work to competitions. Her pottery is exhibited in many museums in the United States and abroad. It is not a Pueblo trait to seek fame or renown. If fame happens, the tendency is to maintain a low profile and play down the events rather than gain notoriety on the pueblo. In 1983 Lucy received two major awards, one from her State and the other from a major institution. Through all the ceremonies she remained quiet but smiling, graciously accepting the applause of the audiences.

A complete list of awards is difficult to make because records are not considered important. Lucy's youngest daughter is keeper of certain treasures in addition to the cows. Scrapbooks filled by various members of the family with old photographs, blue ribbons, certificates, clippings from newspapers, often undated, indicate the variety of honors and were loaned to me for a short time.

The following record, procurred from those books, cannot be complete and may not even be exact, but it indicates the major events.

1950—At the 29th Intertribal Indian Ceremonial at Gallup, New Mexico, Lucy received a Certificate of Merit for achievement and a blue ribbon for an exceptional fine-line decorated jar.

1956, 1957, 1959, 1960, 1961, 1963—Certificates of Merit and blue ribbons. A newspaper clipping from 1957 says, "There are only three full-time potters left at Acoma pueblo." This statement was prior to Lucy's resounding influence, which caused nearly every woman and some men to become potters at Acoma.

1956—The Maria Martinez Special Award, at the Santa Fe Fiesta, with prize money.

1958—The Indian Art Fund Award, announced by renowned photographer Laura Gilpin, chairman of the Fund, in Santa Fe.

On this occasion Laura Gilpin took Lucy to the Laboratory of Anthropology of the Museum of New Mexico to meet Kenneth Chapman. At the museum she was surprised to see some of her own work, which they had collected. She also viewed old Acoma pots and prehistoric corrugated and black-on-white wares, probably for the first time.

1958—First Award, 7th Annual Amer-Indian Art Exhibition, Los Angeles, California.

1960—First Prize, Southwest Association on Indian Affairs.

1961—First Prize, Indian Market, Santa Fe, "for a large undecorated storage jar."

1961—Research prize, Indian Arts Fund of the School of American Research, "for overall excellence."

1967—Six First Prizes, five Second Prizes, two Third Prizes, the Intertribal Indian Ceremonial, Gallup.

1972—First Award, Scottsdale National Indian Arts Council.

1974—"Pueblo Pottery" Exhibition at the Maxwell Museum of Anthropology, University of New Mexico, includes Lucy's work.

1975—First one-man exhibition: "A Tribute to Lucy M. Lewis, Acoma Potter," Museum of North Orange County, Fullerton, California, curated by John E. Collins.

1977—Lucy is invited to the White House.

1982—"Salute to Acoma Potters: Lucy Lewis and Marie Chino," the Wheelwright Museum, Santa Fe.

1982—Driscoll Gallery, Denver, Colorado compiled an Indian art exhibition to go to the Peoples' Republic of China; includes pots by Lucy Lewis.

1983—The Governor of New Mexico Award for Outstanding Personal Contribution to the Art of the State, presented in Santa Fe Capitol Rotunda. Lucy's son Ivan made a formal acceptance speech.

1983—Woman of Achievement award, Northwood Institute, Houston, Texas; a four-day celebration with many honors. Lucy's son Andrew assisted in the acceptance.

MODERN POTTERS EMERGE
FROM THE PAST

IT MAY BE ADVANTAGEOUS TO READERS to have a brief resume of the early prehistory of the American Southwest. One widely accepted definition of this region is the territory that extends east and west between Las Vegas, New Mexico, and Las Vegas, Nevada and north and south between Durango, Colorado, and Durango, Mexico. A southern border assigned so deep in Mexico reflects that "Many anthropologists regard the American southwest as a northern extension of Mesoamerica and argue that any separation of the two is merely a matter of convenience (Dittert and Plog, 1980: 5; *see* Di Peso, 1974: 48–49). The Greater Southwest includes adjoining culture areas in California.

Over this wide territory, people wandered for twelve thousand years. They spread over the deserts, river valleys to mountain heights, and onto the grassy plains and plateau regions. These earliest peoples lived in small nomadic bands and were dependent upon hunting and gathering for sustenance. During the early epochs few areas were occupied for more than one or two hundred years. Slow, continuous changes in population density occurred.

About nine thousand years ago, those who killed large animals for their main food, the "Big Game Hunters," gradually withdrew from the Southwest, following the mammoth and, later, the bison, to the Great Plains. Other bands began moving into the area—peoples accustomed to giving greater attention to plant foods and smaller game. Since plants dictate a less mobile style of life, it followed that small family groups increasingly sought seasonal foods at the height of their productivity and maturity. The lands of northern Mexico and along the present southern New Mexico and Arizona borders were ideal for such purposes. Consequently, a great influx of peoples poured in from northwest Mexico, from west of the lower Colorado River, and later from the Great Basin—the Nevada region. A primitive type of maize appeared in the Southwest between four and five thousand years ago, and its cultivation, between 300 B.C. and A.D. 1, allowed communities to settle in one place.

A summary of accepted ideas regarding the later prehistoric cultures and also the historic period is found in the Lucy's Heritage section in this book, so I will turn my attention directly to Acoma.

> The Acoma tribe resides in its aboriginal location sixty miles west of Albuquerque, New Mexico. The reservation is composed of three primarily residential communities—'á-k'u (Acoma, the old village on the mesa), tí čh íná (a farming village in 'north valley,' which was renamed Acomita by the Spanish), and tí číyâ ma (a farming village in 'north pass,' which was renamed McCartys by the Atchison, Topeka, and Santa Fe railway), while 'á·k'u was the original permanent village of the tribe, it has become more of a ceremonial home in the twentieth century. However, there are a handful of families who by official appointment or on a voluntary basis annually alternate in residence on the mesa. Almost every family on the reservation maintains an individual house or clan home at 'á·k'u" (Garcia-Mason, 1979: 450).

The above source also states:

> The Acoma ancestors comprise four groups of people, one of which had inhabited the Pueblo since early prehistoric times and another who came in around A.D. 1300 from the Mesa Verde area. The other two are believed to have migrated from the Cebollita region (Ruppe 1953). Prehistorically, Acoma province included the occupation within a broad area from the Rio Grande west to the El Morro area. There is evidence that during the thirteenth century, including the period of the Great Drought (1276–1299), the province received a number of migrations. Many ruins of villages formerly inhabited by the Acoma tribe are found in the Los Vetedos and Los Pilares areas (1979: 454).

It was recorded by Adolph F. Bandelier in 1982 that, insofar as he could make out, "the gist of Acoma folklore assigns the origin of the tribe to a separation . . . from the tribe of Cia (Zia) [a Keres-speaking group living along Highway S. 44, about midway between Albuquerque and Cuba, New Mexico]. Thence they drifted to the southwest across the bleak and unprepossessing valley of the Rio Puerco, and, dividing into bands, established themselves in pueblos of small size at the right and left of the Canada de la Cruz, and on the mesa above Acomita, twelve miles north of their present village."

When we begin to think of modern Indian pottery, we have, however, to give some thought to recent history. We learn that in 1821 a man named Captain William

Becknell decided to make a trip from Missouri to New Mexico and sought the assistance of four companions in arranging a three-wagon assemblage of goods to be freighted to the west. In 1822, those wagons set forth from Franklin, Missouri, "over the thick buffalo grass of what was to become the Santa Fe Trail" (Toulouse 1977: 13). It proved to be an event that had a lasting effect on the New Mexico Indian pueblos.

Traders who followed Becknell's trail, between then and 1880, began transporting commercially made articles such as tin pails, enamelware, and kitchen wares, which came to supplant the use of Pueblo pottery in homes of this region. Between 1880 and 1885, the first railroads traversed New Mexico, with increasing freighting business and replacements for Indian pottery. The Indians were fascinated by the trains, and the travelers were attracted by the Indians and their pottery, or souvenirs, which the pottery-makers displayed. Thereby, a new element entered the Pueblo economy when their productions achieved monetary value.

For a span of years, traditional styles continued to be followed in a number of the pueblos. Then tourist demand for the "curio wares" caused an expansion in ceramic production along the railroad routes—passing through the pueblos of Isleta, Laguna, and Acoma villages, and the towns of Albuquerque and Winslow, Arizona. The potters who gathered at the tracks found that new forms were desired also—things with which Easterners were familiar. Consequently they were accommodated by such items as candlesticks, pitchers, bowls with handles, etc. These could be decorated quickly with little concern for designs and painting skill. Thus, by 1900 only a small amount of pottery was made for Indian use. Being somewhat distant from the railway tracks, Acoma during the 1880–1900 period enjoyed further continuance of traditional pottery forms and decorative designs.

Early in the twentieth century other occurrences began to affect the pottery situation. The Museum of New Mexico was created in Santa Fe, and the School of American Archaeology [now Research] was made its manager. Archaeological excavations in the vicinity were initiated, and prehistoric types of pottery revealed. The Museum became deeply involved in the ever-changing picture of Pueblo pottery-making.

Interested outsiders came to aid the Museum in efforts to improve the quality of Indian ceramics. Through several years it was demonstrated to Pueblo potters that high-quality pieces resulted in higher prices, thus careful workmanship bettered the Indian economy. The Museum sponsored fiestas and fairs, with exhibitions to encourage indigenous arts and crafts among the Indians—to revive old arts and to keep the accomplishments of each pueblo group (and other Indians) as distinct as possible. Markets and business concerns were promoted.

By 1922, sixteen Indian pueblos exhibited their wares in Santa Fe and were awarded competitive prizes. This fair and exhibition drew participants from distant Hopi and from Acoma, as well as from the local pueblos. Acoma potters were listed among the prize winners.

It was also in 1922 that the first Intertribal Indian Ceremonial was held near Gallup, New Mexico. Then and henceforth it has introduced hundreds of thousands of interested people to the beautiful arts and crafts produced by Indians from local pueblos and reservation craftspeople from near and far.

After many years with the Museum/School institution in Santa Fe, Kenneth L. Chapman, himself an artist long interested in Indian art, became associated with the Laboratory of Anthropology in 1927. During the 1930s another pottery revival came to pass among the pueblos.

At Acoma it was noticed that nontraditional concepts first appeared. Some of the potters began to modify the typical designs; some were depicted in unusual color arrangements. These styles were short lived. Some Acoma potters turned to archaeological sources. During the same period, geometric and fine-line patterns became frequent. But at no time were the traditional polychrome designs ever abandoned, nor did they fail to be sought by collectors or other purchasers. Through the 1940s and thereafter active potters have been producing wares that sell well, and their names have become famous.

Among the Acoma potters is the artist with whom this publication is especially concerned, Lucy Lewis. Having been born in Sky City, about 1895, she as a child is said to have mainly taught herself by observing her great-aunt Helice Vallo. She was one of the youthful ones, then, who sold their creations at roadside stands along old Highway 66. Happily for all of us, Lucy continues to make pottery to this day.

As she attained maturity, Lucy was married to Toribio Lewis. She gave birth to nine children, two sons and seven daughters. While she assisted with the family farming and running the home, she continued to make pottery of high quality.

As Lucy perfected her pottery, she attended Indian fiestas, not only in her own pueblo, but those of other pueblos, and the events taking place in Santa Fe, Gallup, and increasing non-Indian centers. During the 1940s she signed her wares simply "Acoma, N. Mex." Much of the pottery for the tourist trade was so signed, or "Sky City, N. Mex." In 1950 she entered some of her pottery at the Inter-Tribal Indian Ceremonial in Gallup. There she was selected for an *Award of Merit* for one of her fine-line vessels. With this honor she was established; she became a sought-after potter, and began to sign her productions. Her skill and fame spread.

This, too, is when I came to know Lucy and to appreciate her workmanship, for it was during a period when I had the privilege of serving as a judge of pottery at the annual Ceremonial in Gallup. Henceforth it was my pleasure to see what Lucy brought forth for exhibit year after year. She consequently won many blue ribbons and lesser ones as well. She continued to win top prizes at events held elsewhere each season.

It was also during these fruitful 1950s that Lucy adopted the production of small pottery figures. Turkeys were first, followed by owls, chickens, roadrunners, turtles, and so on. These were delightful, easy to transport, and very popular.

Among the vessels that she fashioned were some special ones for ceremonial use. At Acoma, pottery is given as gifts by the *katsinas* the Keresan word for supernatural beings and their human personators, and to wooden figures carved to represent them. The latter are not dolls as non-Indians think of them, as "toys."

They are likenesses of a whole array of supernaturals who, through various manifestations, interact between man and his deity; thus they are messengers.

At the Indian Market in Santa Fe, 1958, Lucy was given the Outstanding Exhibit Award and other prizes by the Indian Arts Fund. She was then asked by the eminent photographer Laura Gilpin, chairwoman of the Fund, if she had seen the collection of early Acoma pottery housed at the Laboratory of Anthropology [which became a part of the Museum of New Mexico in 1947]. Lucy replied "no." She had not heard of the Laboratory, nor its storehouse of Indian pottery. Thereupon, Miss Gilpin took her to see the collections and to meet Kenneth Chapman.

The designs and the striking corrugated accomplishment of Hohokam, Mogollan (Mimbres), and Anasazi traditions clearly touched something in her. She quite naturally began incorporating these heirloom features into her masterful achievements. But with all these apparent introductions, Lucy never completely abandoned the polychrome styles that she shared with her kinspeople and other potters.

Just as Lucy had watched her great-aunt make pottery, four of Lucy's daughters gave particular observation to the pottery she was making. They commenced to help her by working the clay, polishing the vessels being made, and doing some of the painting. This led to the beginning of their own pottery making. Naturally, Lucy helped them in their efforts. Finally she told them to do their own work.

Lucy Lewis has participated in exhibits of touring displays shown in embassies in Europe, the Near East, Argentina, and Canada. She has permanent exhibits at the Smithsonian Institution in Washington, D.C., and in collections of several other institutions. Her shows include a long list of states from coast to coast, dating from 1956 to the present time. The very *first* of tributes, however, awarded to Lucy Lewis and her pottery-making daughters occurred in 1974.

In ending this resume, with thanks and appreciation to my colleagues from whom these pages have benefitted, I close with a quotation from Betty Toulouse's outstanding book, *Pueblo Pottery.* As she expresses it: "Pueblo pottery making continues to be the most distinctive, versatile, and long-lived craft of any North American Indian group. It is recognized around the world for its excellence and uniqueness, its marvelous variety and links to tradition. Today, pottery is the hallmark of the living Pueblos, and beyond the cultural upheavals of the present era, pottery will no doubt endure as a symbol of Pueblo vitality and cultural identity" (1977: 10, 12).

Bertha P. Dutton, Ph.D.
Research Associate,
Museum of New Mexico
Santa Fe, New Mexico

12 March, 1984

BIBLIOGRAPHY

Ambler, Richard. *The Anasazi*. Flagstaff: Museum of Northern Arizona, 1977.
  Good photographs of pots and the area; general description of prehistoric Four Corners people and the migrations.

Arnold, David L. "Pueblo Pottery: 2000 Years of Artistry" *National Geographic* v. 162, no. 5, pages 593–605, November 1982.
  Brief history of the craft. Well illustrated. Photograph of Lucy Lewis on p. 604.

Barry, John W. *American Indian Pottery*. Florence, Alabama; Books Americana, 1981.
  Popular, illustrated description of pottery. Works by Lucy Lewis and family on pp. 91–92. Many color photographs.

Benedict, Ruth. "Eight Stories from Acoma," *Journal of American Folklore* 43: 59–87. 1930.
  Includes the legend of the Flaming Horse—the Acoma equivalent of the Golden Fleece.

Boas, Franz. *Keresan Texts*. American Ethnological Society Publications vol. 8, pt. 1, 2, 1928, 1925. Reprint, 1974.
  Origin myth, coyote, twin heroes, and other tales of the Keres collected from 1919–1921. Part 1 is in English, Part 2 is in Keresan.

———. *Primitive Art*. New York: Dover, 1955 (unabridged reprint of the 1927 edition).
  A classic attempt to set North American Indian art in context with arts of other peoples of the world in terms of aesthetics, symbolism, and style.

Bradfield, Wesley. *Cameron Creek Village: A Site in the Mimbres Area in Grant County, New Mexico*. Monographs of the School of American Research, no. 1. Santa Fe, 1931.
  Early report on archaeological excavations at a Mimbres site. Black-and-white photographs of pottery.

Brody, J. J. *Mimbres Painted Pottery*. Albuquerque: University of New Mexico Press, 1977.
  Illustrated, scholarly discussion of Mimbres designs, many of which are now used at Acoma.

Brody, J. J., Catherine J. Scott, and Steven A. LeBlanc. *Mimbres Pottery: Ancient Art of the American Southwest*. New York: Hudson Hills, 1983.
  Up-to-date, well illustrated description of Mimbres pottery.

Broster, John B. and Bruce G. Harrill. *A Cultural Resource Management Plan for Timber Sale and Forest Development Areas on the Pueblo of Acoma*. Albuquerque BIA, 1982.
  Gives archaeological and economic background on Acoma pueblo.

Bunzel, Ruth L. *The Pueblo Potter: A Study of Creative Imagination in Primitive Art*. Columbia University Contributions in Anthropology 8. New York: Columbia University Press, 1929. Reprinted by Dover Books, 1972.
  Emphasis on form and design of Pueblo pottery at Hopi, Acoma, Zuni, and San Ildefonso. A classic of its type.

Carlson, Roy L. *White Mountain Redware: A Pottery Tradition of East-Central Arizona and Western New Mexico*. Anthropological Papers of the University of Arizona, no. 19. Tucson, 1970.
  Many of the prehistoric designs in this monograph are used at Acoma today.

Ceram, C.W. (alias Kurt W. Marek). *The First American*. New American Library, 1972.
  Interesting general view of the roots of the native American, expecially Pueblo culture; photographs.

Chapman, Kenneth M. *Pueblo Indian Pottery*. 2 vols. Nice, France: Szwedzicki, 1933.
  Limited edition of 100 plates illustrating the pottery of the Pueblos. Most pieces can be found in the Indian Arts Fund Collection at the School of American Research, Santa Fe.

———. *The Pueblo Indian Pottery of the Post-Spanish Period*. Laboratory of Anthropology Bulletin. General Series, no. 4. Santa Fe, 1983.
  A short essay on Pueblo pottery since the 1600s.

Chauvenet, Beatrice. *Hewett and Friends*. Sante Fe: Museum of New Mexico Press, 1983.
  Dr. Edgar Lee Hewett, founder of the Museum of New Mexico, the School of American Research, and the San Diego Museum of Man, based in Santa Fe in the early 1900s, was mentor to a few special Indians and a leader of archaeological groups. One of his associates, Kenneth Chapman, took an interest in Lucy in the 1950s.

Collins, John E. *A Tribute to Lucy M. Lewis, Acoma Potter.* Museum of North Orange County. Fullerton, California, 1975.
An exhibit catalog of the Lewis family pottery with brief history of exhibits and shows.

Cosgrove, Harriet S. and Cornelius B. Cosgrove. *The Swarts Ruin, a Typical Mimbres Site of Southwestern New Mexico.* Peabody Museum Papers. Cambridge: Harvard University Press, 1932.
Classic work on the Mimbres, including many illustrations of pottery designs.

Curtis, Edward S. *The North American Indians,* vol. 16, pp. 169-248. Large Plate Supplement. Norwood: Plimton Press, 1926. Reprint New York: Johnson Reprints, 1970.
This volume of the famous series gives a general discussion of Acoma history and ceremonies, with exceptional photographs by Curtis. Large plates Nos. 564-573 are of Acoma pueblo and people taken in 1907.

Curtis, Natalie. *The Indian Book.* New York and London: Harper and Brothers, 1907. Reprint New York: Dover, 1968.
Beautiful old book, musical and narrative songs and legends with a section on Acoma.

Densmore, Frances. *Music of Acoma, Isleta, Cochiti, and Zuni Pueblos.* Bureau of American Ethnology Bulletin, no. 165, 1957. Reprinted by Da Capo Press, New York, 1972.
Transcriptions of Pueblo signs made between 1928 and 1940.

Dillingham, Rick. "Nine Southwestern Indian Potters." *Studio Potter,* vol. 6, no. 1, 1976.
Interviews and photographs of nine potters, including Mary Ann Hampton of Acoma, who mentions learning from Lucy Lewis.

———. "The Pottery of Acoma Pueblo." *American Indian Art,* vol. 2, no. 4 pages 44–51.
Well illustrated description of the history of Acoma pottery with brief description of revival of prehistoric Mimbres and Hohokam designs by Lucy Lewis.

Dittert, Alfred E. and Fred Plog. *Generations in Clay: Pueblo Pottery of the American Southwest.* Flagstaff: Northland Press, 1980.
Catalog for the American Federation of Arts exhibit discussing history of Pueblo pottery from prehistoric to modern times. Illustrated with 150 color and black-and-white photographs.

Douglas, Frederick H. *Pottery of the Southwest Tribes.* Denver Art Museum Leaflet, nos. 69 and 70, 1935.
Brief discussion of Pueblo pottery and how to identify specific pueblos.

———. *Pueblo Indian Pottery Making.* Denver Art Museum Leaflet, no. 6, 1930.
Concise statement on methods, materials, and techniques of Pueblo pottery making.

Dozier, Edward P. *The Pueblo Indians of North America.* New York: Holt, Rinehart, and Winston, 1970.
Covers the history and culture of Pueblo Indians, by an anthropologist who was born in Santa Clara pueblo.

Dutton, Bertha P. *American Indians of the Southwest.* Albuquerque: University of New Mexico Press, 1975 (revised edition of *Indians of the Southwest*).
Brief history of cultural traits for each tribe and pueblo.

———. "Pots Pose Problems." *El Palacio,* vol. 73/1, pages 5–15. 1966.
Gives basic definitions of pottery features with specific Southwestern examples.

Dutton, Bertha and Caroline Olin. *Myths and Legends of the Indians of the Southwest.* San Franxcisco: Bellerophen Books.
Stories and ceremonials; Acoma legends, particularly the Shipap origin myth.

Eggan, Fred R. *Social Organization of the Western Pueblos.* Chicago: University of Chicago Press, 1950.
Contains a chapter on Acoma (pp. 223–252) describing kinship, clans, and ceremonial organization.

Ellis, Florence Hawley. *Field Manual of Prehistoric Pottery Types.* University of New Mexico Bulletin, no. 291. Albuquerque, 1950.
Contains culture groups, description of styles, designs, colors, and construction.

———. "On Distinguishing Laguna from Acoma Polychrome." *El Palacio,* vol. 73, no. 3, pp. 37–39. 1966.
Ellis distinguishes the two using temper and design as diagnostic traits.

Ferguson, Erna. *Dancing Gods.* Albuquerque: University of New Mexico Press, 1957.
Elegant descriptions of Pueblo dances and ceremonials, illustrated with 16 paintings by well-known Anglo artists of the twenties.

Fewkes, Jesse Walter. *Additional Designs on Prehistoric Mimbres Pottery.* Smithsonian Miscellaneous Collections, vol. 76, no. 8. Washington, 1924.
Gives additional Mimbres designs. Illustrated.

———. *Archeology of the Lower Mimbres Valley.* Smithsonian Miscellaneous Collections, vol. 63, no. 10, pp. 1–60. Washington, 1914.
Illustrated with black-and-white photographs of Mimbres pottery.

———. *Designs on Prehistoric Pottery from Mimbres Valley, New Mexico.* Smithsonian Miscellaneous Collections, vol. 74, no. 6. Washington, 1923.
Illustrated.

Forde, C. Daryll. "A Creation Myth from Acoma." *Folklore,* vol. 41, pp. 370–387. 1930.
Obtained from an old man who was visiting Washington in 1928. See Stirling for more complete version.

Fox, Robin. *The Keresan Bridge: A Problem in Pueblo Ethnology.* London School of Economics Monographs on Social Anthropology, no. 35. London: Athlone Press, 1967.
Describes Keresan social structure, based primarily on Eggan and Lange, with Cochiti as a case study.

Frank, Larry and Francis H. Harlow. *Historic Pottery of the Pueblo Indians 1600–1800.* Boston: New York Graphic Society, 1974.
Excellent photographs and discussion of pottery by time and region.

Garcia-Mason, Velma. "Acoma Pueblo." In: *Handbook of North American Indians,* Alfonso Ortiz, ed. pp. 450–466. Washington: Smithsonian Institution, 1979.
The author, who is from Acoma, gives an overview of the language, environment, and history of the pueblo. Illustrations include Lucy Lewis pottery (p. 461).

Gill, Robert R. "Ceramic Arts and Acculturation at Laguna." In: *Ethnic and Tourist Arts,* Nelson H. H. Graburn, ed. Berkeley: University of California Press, 1976.
Points out pressures of tourism on contemporary Laguna pottery.

Graburn, Nelson H. H. (ed.). *Ethnic and Tourist Arts: Cultural Expressions from the Fourth World.* Berkeley: University of California Press, 1976.
A collection of papers on the effects of tourism on ethnic arts. Gives a world-wide perspective. Chapters by Brody and Gill pertain to Acoma-Laguna pottery.

Gunn, John M. *Schat-chen, History, Traditions and Narratives of the Queres Indians of Laguna and Acoma.* Albuquerque: Albright and Anderson, 1917.
Gives some of the origin legends and myths of the Acoma.

Guthe, Carl E. *Pueblo Pottery Making.* New Haven: Yale University Press, 1925.
Pottery making techniques as typified by San Ildefonso pueblo are thoroughly investigated.

Harlow, Francis H. "Glazed Pottery of the Southwest." *American Indian Art,* vol. 2. no. 1, 1976.
Includes illustrations of early Acoma glaze painted pottery.

———. *Matte-Paint Pottery of the Tewa, Keres, and Zuni Pueblos.* Santa Fe: Museum of New Mexico Press, 1973.
A detailed description of pottery types from the period 1650–1920.

———. *Modern Pueblo Pottery: 1880–1960.* Flagstaff: Northland Press, 1977.
Well-illustrated description of pottery in each of the pueblos showing developments since the coming of the railroad.

Harrington, J. P. "Haako, Original Form of the Keresan Name of Acoma." *El Palacio,* vol. 56, pp. 141–144, 1949.
According to Harrington, "Akome" means "person from Acoma"; Spanish, Navajo, and Zuni forms of the word are given, but no translation is offered for "Haako."

Jacka, Jerry. *Pottery Treasures: The Splendor of Southwest Indian Art.* Text by Spencer Gill. Portland: Graphic Arts Center, 1976.
Beautiful photographs, including one of Lucy Lewis making pottery (p. 40). Her pottery is pictured on p. 57.

Judd, Neil M. *The Material Culture of Pueblo Bonito.* Smithsonian Miscellaneous Collections, no. 124. Washington, 1954.
Detailed archaeological account of the excavations of Pueblo Bonito, Chaco Canyon, with chapter on pottery.

Kabotie, Fred. *Designs from the Ancient Mimbrenos with a Hopi Interpretation.* San Francisco: Grabhorn Press, 1949 (reprinted by Northland Press, 1982).
The author, a Hopi artist, gives his interpretation of Mimbres designs drawn from Fewkes, Bradfield, and Nesbitt.

Lange, Charles H. "The Keresan Component of Southwestern Pueblo Culture." *Southwestern Journal of Anthropology,* vol. 14, no. 1, pp. 34–50, 1958.
The author points out similarities between Acoma, Hopi, and Zuni architectural features.

Lange, Charles H. and Carroll L. Riley. *The Southwestern Journals of Adolph F. Bandelier.* 4 vols. Albuquerque: University of New Mexico Press, 1966.
Volume 1 contains a report of Bandelier's visit to Acoma in the 1880s (pp. 283–310).

LeBlanc, Steven A. *The Mimbres People, Ancient Pueblo Painters of the American Southwest.* London: Thames and Hudson, 1983.
General work on the Mimbres culture. 129 illustrations.

LeFree, Betty. *Santa Clara Pottery Today.* School of American Research Monograph, no. 29. Albuquerque: University of New Mexico Press, 1975.
Technological study of pottery making based on three Santa Clara families. Illustrated.

Lemos, Pedro J. "Marvelous Acoma and its Craftsmen." *El Palacio,* vol. 24, pp. 234–244, 1928.
Mentions Juana Aragon making excellent pottery in the 1920s.

Lister, Robert H. and Florence C. Lister. *Anasazi Pottery: The Centuries of Prehistoric Ceramic Art in the Four Corners Country of the Southwestern United States.* Albuquerque: University of New Mexico Press, 1978.
A well-illustrated catalog of the Earl H. Morris Memorial pottery collection in the University of Colorado Museum.

Lummis, Charles F. *The Land of Poco Tiempo.* New York: Scribner, 1893 (reprinted by Scribner, 1928).
Chapter 3, "The City in the Sky," gives Lummis' impressions of Acoma in the 1890s, and a brief history of the pueblo.

Mails, Thomas E. *The Pueblo Children of the Earth Mother.* 2 vols. Garden City: Doubleday, 1983.
The culture, crafts, and ceremonials of the Pueblo Indians. Profusely illustrated.

Manley, Ray. *Southwestern Indian Arts and Crafts.* Tucson: Ray Manley Photography, 1975.
Richard Howard's article on pottery notes Lucy Lewis using Mimbres designs on her pottery since the 1950s.

Matson, Frederick R. *Ceramics and Man.* Viking Fund Publications in Anthropology, no. 41. New York, 1965.
A series of papers giving a worldwide perspective on the contribution of ceramic studies to archaeological and ethnological research.

Maxwell Museum of Anthropology. *Seven Families in Pueblo Pottery.* Albuquerque: University of New Mexico Press, 1974.
Catalog of exhibition that featured the Lewis family as one of seven pottery making families.

Mera, Harry P. *The Rain Bird, a Study in Pueblo Design*. Laboratory of Anthropology Memoirs, vol. 2. Santa Fe, 1927. Reprinted under the title: *Pueblo Designs* by Dover Publications, New York, 1970. *Mera traces the rain bird design through various pueblos, including Acoma.*

———. *Style Trends of Pueblo Pottery in the Rio Grande and Little Colorado Cultural Areas from the 16th to the 19th Century*. Laboratory of Anthropology Memoirs, vol. 3. Santa Fe, 1939. *Mera describes early forms of Acoma pottery such as Hawikuh and Ashiwi with fine illustrations.*

Mickey, Barbara (Harris). "Acoma Kinship Terms." *Southwestern Journal of Anthropology*, vol. 12, no. 3, pp. 249–256, 1956. *Compares Acoma kinship terms with those gathered by Kroeber, White, and Parsons.*

Miller, Wick R. *Acoma Grammar and Texts*. University of California Publications in Linguistics, no. 40. Berkeley and Los Angeles, 1965. *Miller used several members of the Lewis family as linguistic consultants in this book. Extremely technical.*

———. "Some Notes on Acoma Kinship Terminology." *Southwestern Journal of Anthropology*, vol. 15, no. 2, pp. 179–184. 1959. *Miller points out similarities and differences between Acoma and Laguna kinship terms, as well as between male and female egos.*

Minge, Ward Alan. *Acoma, Pueblo in the Sky*. Albuquerque: University of New Mexico Press, 1976. *The author traces the social, economic, and political history of the Acoma people from 1540 to the present.*

Nesbitt, Paul H. *The Ancient Mimbrenos, Based on Investigations at the Mattocks Ruin, Mimbres Valley, New Mexico*. Logan Museum Bulletin, no. 4. Beloit College, 1931. *An archaeological report with some interesting photographs of Mimbres materials, including several rare polychrome bowls.*

Oleman, Minnie. "Lucy Lewis: Acoma's Versatile Potter." *El Palacio*, vol. 75, no. 2, pp. 10–12, 1968. *Brief biography with photograph of Lucy Lewis making pottery; mentions Indian Arts Fund award in 1958.*

Ortiz, Alfonso. *Handbook of North American Indians Vol. 9: Southwest*. Washington. Smithsonian Institution, 1979. *An encyclopedic summary of prehistoric and historic Pueblo Indians with chapter on each of the pueblos, including Acoma.*

———. (ed.). *New Perspectives on the Pueblos*. Albuquerque: University of New Mexico Press, 1972. *Articles by a number of authors, based on a seminar held at the School of American Research, Santa Fe.*

Peterson, Susan. *The Living Tradition of Maria Martinez*. Tokyo: Kodansha International, 1977. *Well-illustrated account of Maria and her pottery making tradition.*

———. "Matriarchs of Pueblo Pottery." *Portfolio*. pp. 50–55, Nov./Dec. 1980. *Brief, illustrated article on Maria Martinez, Lucy Lewis, Margaret Tafoya, and Fannie Nampeyo.*

———. *Master Pueblo Potters*. New York: ACA Gallery catalog, 1980. *Introduction by Hamaki Highwater; description of Maria and Santana Martinez, Lucy Lewis, Fanny and Priscilla Nampeyo pottery with photographs of masterworks.*

Ruppe, Reynold J. and Alfred E. Dittert, "Acoma Archaeology: A Preliminary Report of the Final Season in the Cebolleta Mesa Region, New Mexico." *El Palacio*, vol. 60, pp. 259–274, 1953. *Brief archaeological report of excavations at Acoma.*

Ruppe, Reynold J. and Alfred E. Dittert, Jr. "The Archaeology of Cebolleta Mesa and Acoma Pueblo: A Preliminary Report Based on Further Investigation." *El Palacio*, vol. 59, pp. 191–217, 1952. *Postulates continuous occupation of Cebolleta Mesa by ancestors of modern Acoma and withdrawal to mesa top in late P III times (A.D. 1200–1300).*

Schroeder, Albert H. *Southwestern Ceramics: A Comparative Review*. Arizona Archaeologist, no 15. Albuquerque, 1982. *Overview of Southwestern ceramic development, based on a seminar held at the School of American Research, Santa Fe.*

Sedgwick, Mary K. *Acoma, the Sky City, a Study in Pueblo Indian History and Civilization.* Cambridge: Harvard University Press, 1926. Reprinted 1972.
A general history of the pueblo, containing a chapter on pottery.

Shepard, Anna O. *Ceramics for the Archeologist.* Carnegie Institution Publication, no. 609. Washington, 1936.
Basic definition of ceramics and review of clay structure. Very technical.

Snodgrass, O. T. *Realistic Art and Times of the Mimbres Indians.* El Paso: O. T. Snodgrass, 1975.
A discussion of Mimbres art with 262 illustrations of pottery designs.

Spicer, Edward H. *Cycles of Conquest: The Impact of Spain, Mexico, and the United States on Indians of the Southwest 1533–1969.* Tucson: University of Arizona Press, 1962.
Gives a general overview of the history of the Pueblos and the effects of European contact.

Stirling, Matthew W. *Origin Myth of Acoma and other Records.* Bureau of Ethnology Bulletin, no. 135. Washington, 1942.
Gives a long account of the origin legend and a brief description of customs of Acoma.

Stubbs, Stanley. A. *Bird's Eye View of the Pueblos.* Norman: University of Oklahoma Press, 1950.
Gives brief description, aerial photograph and plan of the pueblos as of 1950.

Tanner, Clara Lee. *Arizona Highways Indian Arts and Crafts.* Phoenix: Arizona Highways, 1976.
Chapter by Richard Spivey on pottery notes revival of prehistoric designs on Acoma pottery by Lucy Lewis. Beautiful photographs.

———. *Prehistoric Southwestern Craft Arts.* Tucson: University of Arizona Press, 1976.
Chapter on pottery gives good background on history of technique and design. Well illustrated.

———. *Southwest Indian Craft Arts.* Tucson: University of Arizona Press, 1968. Reprinted 1975.
Well-illustrated, general description of various crafts, including pottery. Mentions Lucy Lewis on p. 104.

Toulouse, Betty. *Pueblo Pottery of the New Mexico Indians.* Santa Fe: Museum of New Mexico Press, 1977.
Illustrated history of Pueblo pottery with particular emphasis on Santa Fe influences.

Washburn, Dorothy Koster. *A Symmetry Analysis of Upper Gila Area Ceramic Design.* Peabody Museum Papers, vol. 68. Cambridge: Harvard University, 1977.
Presents a systematic method of analyzing ceramic design based on archaeological data from west central New Mexico.

Waters, Frank. *Masked Gods.* Albuquerque: University of New Mexico Press, 1950.
Description of and personal comments on Pueblo dances and symbolism.

White, Leslie A. *The Acoma Indians.* 47th Annual Report of the Bureau of American Ethnology. Washington, 1932. Reprinted by Rio Grande Press, Glorieta, N.M., 1973 with color photographs of modern Acoma.
Contains a historical sketch of Acoma and a description of ceremonies, myths, and tales.

———. "A Ceremonial Vocabulary among the Pueblos." *International Journal of American Linguistics,* vol. 10, pp. 161–167.
White points out that many ceremonial words are not archaic, but instead are borrowed from other groups, or are words changed for rhythmic or poetic reasons.

———. *New Material from Acoma.* Anthropological Papers, no. 32. Bureau of American Ethnology Bulletin, no. 136. Washington, 1943.
Contains an autobiographical account by an Acoma Indian which gives interesting insights into Pueblo history.

———. *Notes on the Ethnobotany of the Keres.* Papers of the Michigan Academy of Science, Arts, and Letters, vol. 30, pp. 557–568, 1944.
Gives the Keresan term and uses of plants, their scientific names, and some native beliefs.

———. *Notes on the Ethnozoology of the Keresan Pueblo Indians.* Papers of the Michigan Academy of Science, Arts, and Letters, vol. 31, pp. 223–243, 1945.
Gives Keresan names and uses of animals and birds.

I N D E X

Color: All color photographs were taken by the author, her daughter Jan Peterson, or Dana Levy, with the following exceptions:

Plate **2**, aerial view of Acoma mesa, by Paul Logsdon

Collections:

School of American Research Collections in the Museum of New Mexico (photographs by Dana Levy): Plates **126**; **127** (cat. #303211); **128** (cat. #299912); **278** (cat. #2777); **289** (cat. #2778); **295** (cat. #1120); **308** (cat. #2780); **311** (cat. #2946); **330** (cat. #2968a); **331** (cat. #2977).

Southwest Museum, Los Angeles: Plates **137** (cat. #421G212), George Wharton James Collection; **138** (cat. #30L18), A.C. Vroman Collection; **139** (cat. #457G163), Charles F. Lummis Collection; **140** (cat. #1863G2); **141** (cat. #421G365) George Wharton James Collection.

Sam and Alfreda Maloof: jar on jacket front

Balene Gallery, Houston, Texas; Plate **153**

Dr. Bernard Berman: Plate **159**

Mr. and Mrs. David Schwarz: Plate **312**

Rick Dillingham: Plate **305**

Dr. and Mrs. Paul Harnly: Plate **309**

The author: Plates **306, 334, 335, 337, 351**

Black-and-White: All black-and-white photographs were taken by the author or Dana Levy, with the following exceptions:

Family pictures were lent by Lucy Lewis, Emma Lewis Mitchell, Dolores Lewis Garcia, Belle Lewis Lucero, and Andrew Lewis. Plates **49, 50,** and **52** are by Laura Gilpin; Plates **61** and **62** are by Susan Grnett.

Albuquerque Museum Photoarchives: Plates **23, 26, 30, 33, 34** (**26** and **34** attributed to W.H. Jackson, 1900)

The Library of Congress, Edward S. Curtis Archives (from the published volumes of Edward S. Curtis, 1826): Plates **24, 25, 28, 29, 35**

Museum of the American Indian, Heye Foundation: Plates **27, 31, 32**

Collections:

Museum of New Mexico Collections: Plates **124** (cat. #20102/11); **125** (cat. #20175/11); **136** (cat. 20318/11); **142** (cat. #20167/11); **143** (cat. #43323/11)

School of American Research Collections in the Museum of New Mexico (photographs by Arthur Taylor): Plates **147** (cat. #8317/11); **155** (cat. #8440/11)

Department of Library Services, American Museum of Natural History: Plates **130–135**, Osborn Collection

Museum of the American Indian, Heye Foundation: Plates **144** (specimen #20/8584); **145** (specimen #6/7156); **146** (specimen #24/3196); **148** (specimen #24/3198); **149** (specimen #24/3194)

Department of the Interior, Indian Arts and Crafts Board: Plates **301** (cat. #W.57.9.2); **302** (cat. #W.63.12.7); **303** (cat. #W.66.78.2); **304** (cat. #63.12.8)

Color paintings of Lucy's pottery designs were made expressly for this book by Andrew Lewis; Stanley Lucero (Morningstar Graphics) made drawings of Lucy's designs; and Lucy's grandchildren—Kathy, Claudia, Chris, Adam, and Merle—contributed sketches of their grandmother's patterns they most liked. Though only a small number could be included in the book, the author is grateful for these rewarding contributions and for the warmth and consideration that inspired them.

The rendering of the map of Sky City is after a much-published one by Richard Sandoval. The author appreciates his permission.

定価10,000円
in Japan